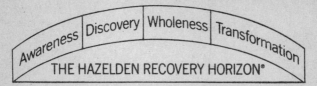

Awareness | Discovery | Wholeness | Transformation

THE HAZELDEN RECOVERY HORIZON®

Just as life is no straight-edged path, so in recovery are we faced with a lifelong journey of hills to climb and valleys to descend. One constant is that we take a searching look at where we've been, where we are now, and where we're going; our focus changes from awareness of a problem, to discovery of solutions, to the wholeness we can enjoy when solutions bring peace, to the kinds of transformations that change us at the deepest levels of our beings.

Awareness to *Discovery* to *Wholeness* and *Transformation*. The Recovery Horizon is Hazelden's commitment to supporting you no matter where you are in your own process of personal and spiritual growth.

DISCOVERY

Moving forward, always on the road to recovery, we discover more about the people we were before dysfunction or addiction became a part of our lives. New and confusing emotions fill our minds and hearts, but as we continue to work, we practice new living skills and explore ways to create different relationships, as a new self emerges.

FROM ANGER TO FORGIVENESS

Earnie Larsen

with

Carol Larsen Hegarty

A HAZELDEN® BOOK
BALLANTINE BOOKS • NEW YORK

Editor's note

Hazelden Educational Materials offers a variety of information on chemical dependency and related areas. Our publications do not necessarily represent Hazelden's programs, nor do they officially speak for any Twelve Step organization.

The authors have changed the names of people who've shared their stories in this book to protect their privacy.

Library of Congress Catalog Card Number: 92-90620

ISBN: 0-345-37982-9

This edition published by arrangement with the Hazelden Foundation

Manufactured in the United States of America

First Ballantine Books Edition: November 1992

To the Thursday Night Men's Group for telling the truth and sharing the journey, and to the Monday Night Joy of Living Meeting where smiles are sincere and secrets safe.

Contents

Introduction

People show up at counseling offices and therapy groups for dozens of reasons. Often, they have marriage problems, communication problems, or issues around shame and passivity. Sometimes they've simply become exhausted and are too tired to cope. What they rarely recognize are the unmistakable fingerprints of unresolved anger that are all over the difficulties they carried in the door.

Untold amounts of energy, effort, and money can be wasted—no matter how sophisticated the technique or how supportive the group—as long as that underlying, undetected anger swims around under the surface. It toxifies everything it touches, masquerades behind a dozen different masks, and halts progress on every front.

The good news is that more and more people are undertaking "anger work" to identify and face up to their underground reservoirs of resentment and rage. The bad news is that merely *confronting* anger is not enough. Many who have bravely followed this path are angrier now than when they started. They simply didn't go far enough. They didn't know that they had only half completed the fundamentally spiritual journey that leads beyond anger to forgiveness.

"Forgiveness work" can only begin when we realize that we have as much right to serenity and happiness as we do to our righteous anger. But there is a consequence in opening Pandora's box, just as there has been a consequence from sitting on the lid. Just letting out the ugly trolls doesn't send them away; it puts us face-to-face with them. It is the *next* leg of the journey, the one that leads from anger to forgiveness, that ends in the garden of serenity.

Forgiveness is not a gift we give to others, but one we give to ourselves. The question is not about whether or not "they" deserve it, but whether or not *we* deserve spiritually whole lives. Forgiveness begins with an act of will, a decision to be victor rather than victim.

As before all journeys, care must be taken to be sure that we understand the terrain and have a clear itinerary. The journey from anger to forgiveness is a bumpy ride, but it's worth it because the destination is worth it. And most of all, *we're* worth it.

1 ✧ ✧ ✧

Faces of Anger

If this is not the golden age of the self-help movement, it's hard to imagine what would be. Anyone interested in self-improvement or enlightened self-management of difficulties that range from codependency and inner child or adult child issues to shame and low self-esteem can find educational material nearly everywhere. And beyond all the print and audio material, there are seminars, college classes, treatment centers, programs, and self-help groups of every imaginable description. A friend recently commented that never before have there been so many opportunities to spill the beans.

The point of all this self-improvement activity obviously goes beyond mere bean spilling, however. *The goal is freedom.* The purpose is to find a way to shuck off the debilitating, painful issues that ride so many with their sharp spurs. And this is the problem for many people involved in the self-help movement: Where is the payoff? Where is the freedom?

Relief Versus Healing

By now, the enormous and still growing self-help movement has acquired enough history to provide a context for us to examine. A common sentiment we hear from people is gratitude for all they have gained, yet frustration at still being stuck so far short of their goals. People frequently talk about the difference between *relief* and *healing*. *Relief* is the experience of finding some measure of peace, even euphoria, at discovering that there is a safe place to talk; that there are people who care and will listen. These are people who have been in the same places and felt the same things. There is even greater relief in knowing that there are steps we can take and principles we can live by that can help ease our discomfort, whether it is as simple as a stone in our shoe or as painful as a sword through our heart. We can find much relief in the self-help movement.

Healing, though, is a different proposition. Healing is the experience of reclaiming something that is missing from within our deepest selves. Healing requires that we treat the cause of our pain rather than simply put on a bandage to protect us from further harm. Healing means not trying to turn away from and erase the past, but in a real way breaking its power: controlling our present-day emotions and responses. Relief and healing are two very different realities.

One woman accurately expressed the predicament by saying, "While I was rowing like mad for shore, I think someone slipped the anchor overboard." Quite a picture! How many of us are rowing madly for shore while an anchor is holding us fast to the ocean bottom? What might that anchor be? For many, what prevents healing and mocks the frantic row to shore is anger that has not given way to forgiveness. The anchor is repressed anger. Forgiveness is the act of pulling the anchor up. In recovery, repressed anger stands in the way of forgiveness like an invisible barrier. We may not even recognize it, but that barrier blocks many of our valiant efforts at self-help. When we can't forgive, we are limiting ourselves. We become fixated on our inability to achieve real intimacy, and we become spiritually stagnant.

Working on Our Anger

Many people claim to have already done extensive "anger work." The adult child movement greatly heightened our awareness of the need for addressing our anger and grief. All too often, though, this anger work only fed an already dancing fire. Many times the result was to make people even more achingly aware of the rage, hurt, and injustice of the past. Many times the anger work stopped right there, and the result was little more than "scab picking." And everyone knows a frequently picked scab will never heal. Even though we can feel great satisfaction in venting our longtime frustration, the journey cannot end there if healing is our goal. The journey from pain to healing is a much longer trip than the journey from pain to temporary relief.

One man told of sneaking into a church one dark night and lambasting God with every insult he could think of. He blamed God for his wife's cancer. He was especially angry since she contracted the disease shortly after he had undergone treatment for alcoholism. In his mind, God should have given him a break after he had "done the right thing." Whatever the validity of this hurting man's theology, his late-night shouting session with God did give him some relief. He said, "It sure felt good to get all that misery off my chest," but it also gave him no small amount of guilt.

The problem with such hit-and-run dealings with anger is that they don't get us anywhere. The relief doesn't last long. Whatever the basic dynamic of anger is or was, it still remains after all the shouting has exhausted us, leaving us hoarse and weak. And, of course, hurling verbal bricks of insults at God or anyone else has nothing to do with forgiveness. So what else is there for us to do but keep rowing for shore, wondering why we never get closer?

Effectively working on our anger takes more than just recognizing that we are angry, although we do need to start with recognition. But we also need a thorough understanding of the dynamic of anger, the manner in which anger is still acting out in our daily lives. Once we've done that, we need to know the steps required to move past our anger to forgiveness. Then, if it is possible or appropriate, we can make an attempt at reconciliation. This full-fledged program is a far cry from merely "picking the scab."

Recognizing Our Anger

One of the most difficult aspects of moving past our anger to forgiveness is that so often we don't see that we are angry. Since it's invisible to us—although usually not to those around us—we take no action against it. The first task then, as always, is for us to know the enemy.

The following twenty-five-question examination may serve as a magnifying glass as you look for the fingerprints of repressed anger that may well be smudging up your life:

1. Are you habitually impatient?
2. Are you often frustrated?
3. Do others seem constantly to "be in your way"?
4. Are you usually on your guard against being cheated?
5. Do you feel a more or less constant pressure to prove yourself?
6. Are you habitually fearful of somehow being "caught"?
7. Does it seem (or feel) that someone is always watching you?
8. Do you secretly resent others' success, feeling that yours is never recognized?
9. Are the negative things in your life more obvious to you than the positive?
10. Do you habitually find a lot to complain about?
11. Do you often feel insecure, believing that others are superior to you?
12. Are you afraid you will end up with less than you need?
13. Do you habitually expect bad things to happen?

14. Is it hard for you to "go with the flow"?
15. Is it often difficult for you to stand up for yourself?
16. Do you secretly believe that your feelings are not important?
17. Do you usually keep your preferences to yourself, often deferring to what others want?
18. Do you feel your needs are often minimized or ignored altogether?
19. Do you have temper tantrums?
20. Do you regularly tend to overreact?
21. Is it hard for you to accept that others care about and love you?
22. Are you frequently afraid that somehow you are "missing out" on what counts?
23. Are you often disrespectful to those with less power than yourself?
24. Does the intimacy of others somehow make you uncomfortable?
25. Are you often sad?

Count your "yes" answers. Multiply that number by four. The closer you are to one hundred, the clearer are the fingerprints of anger on your life, whether or not you're aware of it.

Any unchallenged, unrecognized anger is a powerful core inside us, and its effects reach out in many directions. Repressed anger creates systems which guarantee that we continue the situation that caused our anger in the first place. This is why recognizing our repressed anger is such an important step on our path toward ultimate freedom. The strands that lead us from our present hurt back to its source are easy to miss. Hidden beneath the cover of years, the source of our pain often lies buried, but it is still incredibly potent. It's no accident that "somehow" people marry individuals who enable them to duplicate situations they resented in childhood. It's no accident that, after many years of living, people continue the same patterns, making the same decisions they swore they would never make again. We are incapable of real change when we don't understand the source or power of our old patterns. We don't have a choice about what we don't understand.

If you scored high on the twenty-five questions, how clearly do you see the origins of your anger? How clearly do you see the system of roadways that invariably carry you to the same destinations? How evident is your need for relief and healing from being trapped in this exhausting labyrinth of misery in your life?

Stages of Anger

Most of us have heard the saying, "If it walks like a duck and quacks like a duck, it probably is a duck." This point is true enough. But though anger is anger, not all angry people are in exactly the same place. We may well be in very different stages of dealing with our anger. Following are six different stages we can experience on the journey between anger and forgiveness. Thinking about these stages can help you identify your position on your long walk home to healing.

Angry, but don't know it.

Anger wears camouflage and a variety of masks. All anger doesn't show itself in rageful tantrums and plate throwing. Legions of furious people think they don't have anger issues because they don't blow up or foam at the mouth. But anger may be the strongest dynamic in their lives, and their greatest barrier to happiness.

Angry, and do know it.

Some people fairly reach for the ceiling when the question, "Do any of you feel you have a significant amount of repressed anger?" is asked at a meeting. They know something is wrong. They know all too well there is an angry cauldron burning in their bellies and an aching in their heads.

Angry, but not ready to do anything about it.

Change is essentially a spiritual journey that goes beyond the merely rational or logical. Spiritual changes can't be "decided" or "ordered up." People are ready when they are ready—not before. Many people know or suspect they are angry, but they are not ready to grapple with it. Right now they see their anger as too savage, too dangerous. Or they may still find too much comfort wallowing in the anger, too much sweetness in justifying all the damage that was done to them. And, of course, if they are not ready to deal with the anger, then neither are they ready to deal with forgiveness. Since in all things there is some trade-off, they are opting for the consequence that befalls everyone who will not forgive: resentment.

Angry, and ready to do something about it.

These folks have passed over the first two hurdles toward the freedom of forgiveness. They have recognized their anger and have risen above all the reasons to stay caught in that anger. These people are on their way to healing.

Ready to do the work, but don't know how.

Such people are champing at the bit to get rid of their anger, but they don't know what to do. They may not even know there is such a thing as "anger work." Perhaps they are discouraged by seeing others who have done ineffective anger work and who appear to be more damaged than before they started. Yet they know their anger is an unacceptable barrier to progress. But how do they start? What do they do? Where do they begin?

On the journey, but moving slowly.

There are those who have moved down the path toward forgiveness but aren't there yet. Life is a continuous process. Progress, not to mention arriving at the goal, is never instantaneous. The journey from anger to forgiveness is extremely hard work, but justified by achieving the goal. For those people who decide to continue the journey, a great reward awaits.

The Chain Reaction

Repressed anger is an issue that must be addressed by the vast majority of people who seek recovery and freedom. The journey begins when we first come to recognize the various faces of anger we may be wearing in our lives and the resulting indecision they create.

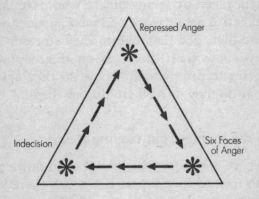

Look at this triangle and visualize the chain reaction that starts with repressed anger. When you think about it, this process is inevitable. Every person who is an adult child, who is codependent, who is shame-based, or who has a low self-esteem has anger issues! It couldn't be any other way. And, over the years, a good bit of that anger gets submerged and repressed. Perhaps we no longer even recognize its virulence in our lives. But that doesn't mean that the anger has gone away.

On the lower right side of the triangle are the six faces of anger. They are:

- Depression
- Smoldering Rage
- The Fidgets
- Secret Keeper
- Victim
- Switched Addictions

These are the *expressions* of repressed anger that reveal themselves whether we are aware of them or not. Anger isn't always expressed in temper tantrums, by throwing things around, or in other forms of overt rage. There are much more subtle ways to show repressed anger. All six faces of anger will be discussed in detail later in this chapter.

On the lower left side of the triangle is indecision. This represents the point at which we are stuck. Perhaps we have not made a liberating decision to change because of our delusion or denial about our anger, or because of some unexamined myths we have about anger itself. Maybe we are not even aware that there are decisions to be made about our anger. Regardless of the reason, we don't take action against the anger that keeps us right where we are.

So the triangle is complete. We are stuck with our repressed anger, evidenced by our different expressions of it, and we are thus unwilling or unable to make a new decision. This inability to decide or control our lives leads to more repressed anger. The chain reaction keeps going because whatever we don't understand can easily control us.

Here are two stories from real people's lives that show the chain reaction caused by repressed anger. The process represented by the triangle was unknown to both of them, so it kept them anchored in their anger. The woman represents the "victim" face of anger and the man represents the "switched addictions" face of anger. See if their experiences translate into your own life.

Kim's Story

One of the women in a self-help group—we will call her Kim—always seemed to have a chip on her shoulder. She was emotionally withdrawn, had a great deal of trouble sharing her feelings, and often seemed to be at war with the world. Her body language, the look in her eye, and the tone of her voice were all hostile. But Kim was sincerely trying to recover from a primary addiction, and her life had gotten better. There is no question about that. She had made some very dear friends in this group, yet she didn't have that vital sense of freedom. She didn't begin to make progress until she began to share her repressed anger with the rest of the group. Then it became quite clear to her (and to everybody in the group) that she had been the victim of some abuse as a child. Until now, she had not fully understood or acknowledged the depth of that abuse. Yet the more Kim talked, the clearer it became that her parents were emotionally unavailable for her and that she had learned from her family to protect herself at all times.

Since the primary abuse she felt was from her father, Kim had deeply internalized the perception that all men are abusive and would hurt her if she gave them a chance. "Victim" became her negative self-definition. She developed a thick emotional wall between her and all men. That wall had caused her a lifetime of disappointment and heartbreak. *Of course* there was anger there!

Anger is always about injustice, perceived or real; it is the emotional response to injustice. In the past, whenever we felt we were not getting what was coming to us, whenever we felt we were getting cheated or short-changed, whenever we were made to do things that weren't fair (like apologize when we weren't wrong), we felt plenty of anger! When we were forced to shut up when we had something to say, when we were punished for legitimate feelings—even as small children—we knew somehow that we were being punished unfairly. *Whenever injustice happens, anger also happens.* And just because some of these events may be twenty, thirty, even forty years old does not mean these events are not still controlling our lives.

Kim hadn't acknowledged all her anger, but she was unknowingly wearing the face of anger called *victim.* Her habitual attitude was, "Look what the world is doing to me now! I never have any luck. I don't have a chance to make the choices that would finally make me equal with other people." She was giving away a lot of power by thinking this way. She had an enormous fear that she could never have a happy relationship. All her energy was used to defend herself from further abuse.

Now think about Kim's situation and the third corner of the triangle, indecision. She was completely unaware that residual childhood anger was so much in control of her life and that it was being expressed in this passive-aggressive, hostile, and victimlike face. Victims don't see themselves as being decision makers, so Kim didn't think she had any decisions to make. With this thought pattern so firmly in place, no matter how much reading she does, no matter how hard she tries to "work her program," no matter how many friends she makes in the group, her improvement will be limited. She is not going to have any freedom because she is still chained to her anchor.

Kim's anchor is not only repressed anger; it's ignorance. She doesn't understand what's going on, and therefore she's not going to decide to do anything to change her situation. Both are keeping her chained to where she is.

Charles's Story

Here's another example. Charles has been in Alcoholics Anonymous (AA) for a long time. He's a beautiful man doing very hard work in recovery. Charles has helped countless other people reach sobriety. He reads a lot of recovery literature, goes to many meetings, and practices the Twelve Step program in all his affairs. Yet Charles has never been able to escape his anger. In his own words, "It's like there is always a big gaping hole in my chest—a missing part of my life. And even though I am grateful for being sober, even though my life is so much better than it was, it still isn't what I want it to be. Somehow, something I need is missing." Then, slowly, he, too, revealed that he came from a very abusive background. In his case, he was emotionally impoverished. He was never shown warmth, never touched, and never complimented. He wasn't recognized or affirmed.

Charles had been a farm child. His life was practically all work with little diversion. No lightness. No balance. His life was different from his schoolmates, and he knew this and resented it. Remember that anger is the response to injustice. So feeling that injustice, he accumulated a great storehouse of repressed anger. Now, for Charles, a *switched addiction* came up as his particular face of anger. When he stopped drinking, he replaced alcohol with work as his problem solver. He told himself, "I know I have this big deficit in the middle of myself. There is a hole there, but certainly with enough money—and the things that money can buy—that hole will be filled up. If I'm successful enough in business, I will achieve the peace of mind and serenity I'm really looking for."

Even though he worked hard to become an extremely successful businessman, no matter how much money he had in the bank, the emptiness remained. Remember, hardly anyone works harder than this man at recovery. In fact, Charles works as hard at recovery as he works at business. He starts groups, he sponsors newcomers, he gives AA talks. There seems to be no limit to what he will do. But his anger is firmly in place, and it's calling all the shots.

The important point is that he's not aware of being eaten up by his anger. He is aware that he is angry, but that's not the same as understanding that a load of repressed anger is poisoning his whole life. He is expressing his angry feelings by being compulsive about work, compulsive about staying busy, always pushing, pushing, pushing to get things done.

Can you relate to Kim and Charles? Is there anything in their stories that is in common with your story? Do you feel that you're anchored *even though* you feel great gratitude for the freedom you've gained and the progress you've made? Is there repressed anger at the top of *your* triangle? How is that anger expressing itself in your life? What are some of the faces of anger that might fit in the right corner of your triangle?

The Faces of Anger

Depression

Depression is probably the most common face of anger. Even if you are not clinically depressed, do you live with a sense of the blues, with negativity? Do you often feel there is a great disaster about to happen? All of these attitudes may now be *habits*, but at their root is likely to be anger that you never recognized, never dealt with adequately, never processed emotionally. Intellectualizing won't do it. We may very well *know what caused our pain*, but if we don't deal with the hurt and damage from the past *on an emotional level*, we will be stuck. No matter how many eloquent words we give to "our story," we are still not free of anger if we don't touch it where it lives and operates—deep in our feeling selves.

Can you relate to the depressive face of anger? Having no enthusiasm is a telling symptom. We can't get emotionally involved. We don't feel emotionally "up" even if there is some wonderful event on the horizon—a graduation, a party, or a happy celebration. On a feeling level, nothing makes a difference one way or another. Another symptom might be called "the drags" or simply fatigue. In this case, the smallest task seems to take too much energy. Just getting out of bed becomes a dreaded task. Emotional emptiness. Weakness. Tiredness. The drags.

Another symptom of depression is a tendency to hide and isolate ourselves from others. Except on a very superficial level, we withdraw from people. Even when we make some friends, we find excuses not to be with them. If our friends are going to meet on Wednesday night to go to a play or a movie, we will find a reason to opt out. If some of our friends meet every Saturday to walk around the lake, we might convince ourselves we don't have time to do it or that it's not the best thing to do. We hide and isolate.

Physical problems are yet another symptom of anger's depressive face. If we live with enough anger and enough stress, it may well start to show up as stomachaches or as lower back pain, frequent headaches, constipation, or difficulty digesting our food. All of these are physical messages of psychological and spiritual distress. When our bodies tell us they're hurting, we sometimes need to take a look at our wounded spirits.

Curt's Story

Here's a typical example of the depressive face of anger. For what seemed like many years—but was really only four—Curt was depressed but functional. Being depressed does not always mean you are dysfunctional. Curt was writing books, giving talks, and getting along very well professionally. But at the same time he felt terrible negativity and hostility. He also felt emotionally flat. Chronic fatigue was one expression of his depression, but he didn't know the source was really his anger about personal commitments. Personal commitments had lost meaning for him. Curt had to lie down seven or eight times a day! His first thought in the morning was about when he could get back to bed; he *needed* that much sleep. Being tired all the time really meant he was angry all the time, but he was unaware of it. Until he recognized this many years later, Curt couldn't think clearly about his situation, let alone make an effective decision to do something to change it. Now, in the light of his new understanding, he knows that he was furious. But he was chained down by all his justifications for not making the decisions required to find freedom. He stayed stuck, and his depression got worse. Can you relate to Curt at all?

Smoldering Rage

Another face of anger is called *smoldering rage*. One symptom is the tendency to take everything that happens personally. People with this smoldering rage show it in frequent emotional flare-ups. Smoldering people are unpleasant and can even be dangerous to be around. We don't usually have close friends. We may have terrible problems with intimacy because we don't feel safe to others. We are often prejudiced. In fact, we can be the most inflexible people in the world. We have to be *against* someone; we *need* an enemy.

People with smoldering rage can often be arrogant. We like to have all the answers. Sometimes we are terrible listeners. We might not grant that others have a worthwhile point to be made about anything. This face of anger may show up in our driving habits. If someone cuts in front of us while driving down a highway, we'll tailgate the offender. *Many* people in recovery programs carry this smoldering rage. And no matter how many groups we go to, until we deal with our anger, the anchor will hold us firmly in place.

Mary's Story

Here's an example of smoldering rage. Mary is a woman who at first appeared not to have abuse in her background. A crisis occurred when she was unjustly fired from her job. She was falsely accused of a terrible act of mismanagement and was simply let go. She hadn't been well-liked at work because of her emotional flare-ups, but the specific event of her firing was trumped-up. It really wasn't fair.

Mary was devastated and furious. Remember, anger is always the result of real or perceived injustice. Only after a lot of soul-searching did Mary realize that she had done a lot to sabotage her job. Even though the reason she was fired was not valid, she had made a great contribution to her own downfall. The chip on her shoulder had made her a target. Her dismissal had a lot to do with the morale problem she created in the office. Who wants to be around somebody who may blow up at any given moment? Mary was impatient and arrogant. If something wasn't her idea, it didn't count. Over time, the sparks flying from her repressed anger burned too many people.

Unknown to Mary, there was deeply buried anger and rage about her childhood behind her chronic crankiness and faultfinding. But because she made no choice to change her attitude, her negative feelings always surfaced and set her up for more damage.

Can you relate to this smoldering rage? Think about the way you drive, the language you use, the prejudice that might be in your life. Do you have frequent emotional flare-ups? Are people hesitant to be around you? Are you often alone and isolated and don't know why? No matter how many positive moves you make, if this pattern is firmly in place and you don't deal with it, you are not going to get rid of that anchor.

The Fidgets

Another face of anger is *the fidgets*. People with this behavioral style always seem to be tap dancing faster than everybody else. We have very little serenity. We seem to be always looking over our shoulder as if we are afraid to get caught or blamed for something. People with the fidgets are terrified of commitment. No matter where we go, we've lined up five or six reasons to leave. We need a back door, a way to get out. Fidgety people have trouble with relationships and intimacy. Behind our fear of commitment is a deep fear of vulnerability.

Fidgeters lie—often in the form of half-truths. As a result, daily life becomes unnecessarily complicated. Why? Because we are terrified that somebody is going to get angry with us. Unconsciously, we dread facing a time in the past that taught us that we could never be good enough to feel secure and comfortable. Since making a commitment is experienced as an invitation to disaster, we will do anything to wiggle around a promise. That's why we fidgety people are awfully hard to count on. We often book ourselves for two or three or four things all at the same time. We may agree to be with you at 6:00, but also agree to help our parents move at 6:00, and *also* agree to chair a meeting at

6:00—all on the same day! So we continually put ourselves in a kind of hot box where we can't keep our commitments.

We fidgeters typically have to run to make telephone calls. If we go out to dinner or to a play, we don't have the serenity to just sit there and relax, putting work or telephone calls on the back burner. We can't really enjoy the show or the people we are with. Fidgeters can't do or think about one thing at a time. We're always going in two or three directions at once.

Alice's Story

By working through these symptoms in therapy, one fidgeter named Alice came to understand the relationship between her frenzied life-style and the fact that she never really got "good stuff" at home. She had wanted to go to college, but only her sister was given the opportunity. Alice started working at fourteen years old and to this day, thirty-four years later, nearly every working day of her life has been at jobs she could do blindfolded and with both hands tied behind her back.

Not everyone in her situation would respond the way she did, but Alice's reaction was to dance faster and faster. To complicate matters, this woman has a heart of gold and would do almost anything for you. But the problem is, she will do almost anything for *anybody*—so she's always running 150 miles an hour.

It's not surprising that Alice married a "baby." Fidgeters are notorious for bailing other people out of work or problems or trouble. So *of course* she married somebody who was absolutely dependent upon her. He needed her to be there every second of every day to make their decisions, to pick out their clothes, to cook their meals, to think for him, and often even to act for him.

Burdened beyond belief, Alice had a lot of bottled-up anger that she expressed in this frenetic way. Only when she came to understand this, and only by working a specific program for her anger, was she able to make any changes in her life—to cut herself free of the anchor.

Secret Keeper

Another face anger shows is that of the *secret keeper*. This person must always look good. We secret keepers will lie about our own pain because we don't want to spoil our image. If it is necessary in order to maintain a good front, we'll minimize what hurts. We often apologize, whether we're wrong or not. We'll rationalize or make excuses for ourselves. In a group, we secret keepers may smile when we are talking about the pain in our lives. We may not realize that people who do this are often not respected. Like the victim's face, the secret keeper's face eventually comes across as being false. But if this pattern is firmly in place, if we don't decide to "get real," our anchor of anger never even gets nudged.

To what degree can you relate to the secret keeper? To having to look good? How much delusion and denial is in your life? How much energy and time do you spend tending to the outside, the facade, rather than to the inside, developing depth and some real self-confidence?

Many of us learned to avoid making waves. We heard a lot of things like, "Let's hide this from Dad," or "Don't let anyone know." In short, we learned to keep secrets. We learned that our lives had to be geared around showing a good face to other people. We learned that *seeming* is more important than *being*. So naturally we grew up with a great deal of anger over all that bobbing and weaving. And we made no decision to do something with our anger, so we remained stuck.

Victim

The next face of anger is known as *victim*. Remember Kim, the woman in the first story? We victims feel we have no options. Down deep we sense that we don't count—that no one really takes us seriously. We get no respect. Remember Mary, the woman who got fired for an unjust reason? Because she was so unpleasant to work with, she set herself up as a potential victim.

It is true that victims seldom get respect, and we are seldom taken seriously. The victim mentality sees no options—which eliminates the chance to make positive decisions. By not taking responsibility for our own growth, we victims don't even respect *ourselves*. When we say, "Why are these things always happening to me?" we have a genuine complaint. We *do* get more than our share of hard knocks. But it isn't random luck that's doing this. Most often *we* are doing it to ourselves. People who are afraid to hope are terribly vulnerable. People who are terrified of success will find a way to fail. So awful things do happen to us.

People with victim mentalities often play dumb. It might be embarrassing to think about, but do you or have you ever played dumb? Have you pretended you didn't understand something that really you understood very well? Have you ever been asked about an issue that you had an opinion about—whether it was politics, religion, or a problem at work—but you acted as if you didn't have an opinion at all? This passive behavior may be seen as the opposite of smoldering rage, but at the core of each is still unresolved anger. One acts like a tyrant while the other pretends not to understand. But as different as these behaviors appear on the surface, they're both ways of expressing anger.

Ben's Story

Consider the case of Ben, a seventeen-year-old in a therapy group. He is a perfect example of a victim. Ben was extremely angry at his family, particularly at his father, a recovering alcoholic. Down deep, he was also angry at himself and his own powerlessness. This accumulated frustration played out as Ben withdrew intellectually. He acted as if he weren't very bright; he played at looking dumb. Since he felt that he didn't measure up, he didn't dare test himself. Not surprisingly, Ben hated to be thought of as an airhead, and he resented being treated like a five-year-old child. But he still wouldn't take responsibility for the success or failure of his own life. He wouldn't stand up and take responsibility for anything. So how else could anybody view him except as an irresponsible scatterbrain?

The anger anchor was tying this young man to old unhappiness. Ben wanted to be a happier person. He wanted to be a respected person, but it wasn't happening for him. He was not taking action or making decisions to cause something better to happen. Since he didn't understand the process that was causing him so much pain, he was a victim of his own buried anger.

Switched Addictions

Another face of repressed anger has to do with *switched addictions* or whitewashing some terrible abuse that happened in the past. Many of us are very brave people who are working hard at our recovery. Suppose we have achieved sobriety, but we don't seem to be making the progress we'd dreamed about. Perhaps we do not enjoy serenity—we have no real peace of mind or freedom. What's it all about? Often the problem is either a switched addiction or a long-buried abuse, a hidden trauma in the past that was never dealt with. No one can simply pass over those events. Until we bring them out in the open and deal with them, they hold us down.

A sober alcoholic, for example, might have switched the addiction to some kind of sexual activity. Maybe this person now cannot get along without having two or three sexual encounters in the same day. Or maybe this person enters a relationship completely based on sexual activity. Intimacy may be impossible even to imagine; it's only sex that keeps this person with his or her partner. Or perhaps the switched addiction is to work or money. People often turn their addictive ways to religion or sometimes even to recovery. In any case, the addictive process, with all of its delusion and denial, preoccupation and inflexibility, is still fully active. That's because of the hidden anchor—the trauma that wasn't dealt with. Many times when we seem absolutely stuck, when we start to dig around in the roots of our experience, we come up with crushing memories we didn't even know we had. We are absolutely amazed to find that a terrible event or series of events has been buried alive.

Bob's Story

Bob, another gentleman who was raised on a farm, told of breaking through just such an emotional cocoon. The abuse from his father had been horrendous. He spoke with tears in his eyes of being beaten because as a small boy he was not able to tie hay bundles as quickly or skillfully as his adult uncle did.

Even now, forty years later, he could see him-self at nine years old, out in the field with his uncle, tying up hay bundles. When the gruel-ing day was over, he recalled feeling proud that he had done a man's work. Then his fa-ther came along and looked at the bundles the boy had tied. Of course his work was not perfect like his uncle's. But rather than offer-ing praise and encouragement, his father beat him. And at that point in the story, this fully competent, very successful businessman shook with sobs as he relived the trauma of that terrible abuse.

What has gone on in your life that may cause an anger anchor to be there? As you think through your own life story, is there some kind of hidden trauma in the past that you have never dealt with? Perhaps, very un-derstandably, the situation was so painful that you've pretended it never happened or tried to forget it. Yet for all your recovery efforts, have you only lengthened the chain that binds you to the anchor? Remember that all anger is built around injustice. If there is some kind of hidden trauma in your life, you will certainly be angry. Breaking free of that anchor of repressed anger may require some professional help. It may require getting into a therapeutic group and finding support to help you go back, face, and work through that abuse, finally putting it behind you. Professional support may be necessary. But whatever form the therapy takes, getting free of the anchor means facing facts.

Six Skills for a Happy Life

What does it cost us to hang on to our anger? Let's take a look at the six basic skills a person needs to lead a decent, happy, successful recovering life. As you read, think about how the hidden anger in your life becomes an obstacle to developing and strengthening these skills.

The first skill for successful living is *the ability to establish (correct) goals or direction*. The word *correct* is in parentheses because it means whatever is correct for *you*. There's no benefit in exploring goals and a direction that *someone else* thinks you should be pursuing. Your own goals and direction bring specific meaning and fulfillment into *your* life. Those of us who do not have the ability to identify goals and then to set out in that direction are going to have a hard time achieving successful, happy lives.

But look what happens if we are acting out one of the faces of repressed anger. If we are the victim, for example, we are not going to set meaningful goals or move in an appropriate direction *because we think we don't de-*

serve it. If we are like the secret keeper, who always needs to look good, we are not going to pick the right goals or direction either. We're going to pick something we think is pleasing to someone else. We may have lost confidence in our ability or even our right to make something meaningful happen for ourselves. If we are depressed, we may be losing so much personal power that we may not even be able to *identify* anything meaningful to us, let alone set out and make it happen.

The second basic skill necessary for successful living is *the ability to ask for what you need.* Those of us who cannot ask for what we need are probably not going to get it. What we will get most often is angry. And then what we will get is even. And so we live within the vicious cycle of not asking for what we need, not getting what we need, getting angry, and then getting even. If we are fidgety people, for example, we are not going to stop long enough to ask for what we need. We are too afraid someone will get angry at us. So we either ignore our own needs or cater to everybody else's. Either way, our needs are not met.

The third skill is *patience with life.* Successful living does take patience. A person smoldering with rage is not able to be patient, nor is someone who has switched addictions. Think about the face of anger that seems to fit *you*. Put it in front of any of these success-ful living skills and see what an obstacle it is. That is why so many of us aren't getting on with our recovery and our real freedom, no matter how hard we work.

The fourth skill is *the ability to forgive*. People who cannot forgive themselves and cannot forgive the unfairness of life are not going to feel very peaceful or happy. Anger makes us incapable of forgiving ourselves, life, or anyone else.

The fifth skill is *the ability to enjoy the moment*. Anger precludes enjoying anything. Think about depression, smoldering rage, and frantic fidgeting. Any one of these faces of re-pressed anger keeps us from enjoying our lives. Victims have a hard time enjoying much about life. Secret keepers are not truly happy. Those of us caught in another addic-tion do not fully enjoy our lives either.

The sixth skill is *the creative willingness to repay your debt to the universe*. Truly happy people are contributing something to life. Of-ten they are involved in creating beauty of some kind. Perhaps it's simply by reaching out to a friend in need, writing a letter to a lonely person, or volunteering regularly. Whatever form it takes, they make a con-scious effort to leave the world better than they found it. Anger is too consuming to al-low much creative compassion.

Which face of anger do *you* wear? That face is between you and the rest of the world. Can you see the distortion and the limitation it creates? Match your face of anger against the six successful living skills, and it may become quite obvious why the anchor of repressed anger is so firmly in place in your life.

2 ✧ ✧ ✧

Empowerment Through Understanding

Empowerment through understanding simply means that we can reclaim an enormous amount of power over our own recovery and our own change process if we thoroughly understand what is going on in our lives. Many of us work so hard to make changes happen! We go to a self-help group, read, practice our affirmations, listen to tapes—and yet that hidden anger stays firmly embedded because we don't really recognize what's holding us back. Not that understanding alone makes change; it doesn't. But it does empower us to make the decisions that will make change possible.

Empowerment begins by realizing and accepting that no one else has your answers. Only *you* have your answers. And other people's truth won't do you much good either. The only truth that will make a real difference is your own truth. That means we must learn to take responsibility and begin by facing the facts of our lives for the sake of our own mental machinery. Until we come to understand what is going on inside, our repressed anger remains untouched, protected by indecision. Understanding ourselves promotes direction by moving us out of the realm of magic. Without some real understanding of what's holding us back from empowerment, the only hope we have of improvement relies on some kind of lucky break. Until then, we aren't in control. We have to look to someone or something totally outside of ourselves to make our decisions for us. And that's a terribly deficient position to be in. The following example illustrates this position.

Charlie's Story

Not too long ago, during a gray Minnesota winter, there was a terrible cold snap. The temperature reached thirty degrees below zero. The mechanism on Charlie's electric garage door opener froze up. He knew enough to disengage a chain that was hanging down from the track the garage door runs on. By yanking on the chain, he made the door open manually. So far so good. But later on, when it warmed up, Charlie wanted to hook the chain back up so the garage door would again open automatically. No way in the world! Because he had no understanding of how that mechanism worked, he had no idea how to hook it back up. So once in a while Charlie and his wife would walk by, hit the ON button, and hope for a lucky break. They hoped that magically, somehow, the pieces might fall into place and the garage door would start working again. Their ignorance had doomed them to a powerless, victim mentality. Then one day a mechanically minded friend came over and had the thing fixed in two minutes. He was baffled by Charlie's difficulty. "Well, of course," he said, *obviously* this is what you needed to do." But it wasn't obvious to Charlie because he didn't understand how the garage door opener worked.

When it comes to a garage door, it isn't *vital* to understand its inner mechanisms. We can always get somebody who does understand it to come over and fix it. But when it comes to our *lives*, nobody but us can fix what needs fixing. If we don't take responsibility for ourselves, no one else will. Perhaps the problem will never get fixed, and we may spend the rest of our days hoping against hope for a supernatural lightning bolt. A magic phrase. A magic book. A magic speaker that somewhere down the line is going to say the words that fix us. But that never happens. The responsibility is ours.

Acceptance of Reality

The hidden anchor of repressed anger is partly held down by lack of acceptance. Until we accept the injustice that caused the anger, we cannot be healed. We have no choices to make about a situation we won't accept as real. Perhaps something in us knows that grief and sadness often come hand in hand with acceptance. We correctly sense that acceptance will give entrance to genuinely painful feelings that many of us have been squelching for years. We simply don't *want* to have to face the power of those violent feelings. We've chosen instead to lock the lid and bar the door—no matter what the price.

To put some flesh and blood around this concept, here's an example of a man who was dealing with heavy, long-term depression. Like so many of us, Jerry had been "working" at his recovery but had never become aware of the expression of anger in his life. That's why his divorces, his extreme harshness toward his children, and his generally miserable state of mind were so mysterious to him. He knew very well that something was wrong; every day he lived with the unhappy effects. But he had no idea at all what the *cause* might be. Now, as you read Jerry's story, it may seem extreme. You may want to disassociate yourself from his situation. But the idea is not to compare his situation with yours. Comparison isn't the point. The point is to understand and to see the dynamic, the process that's involved. What's causing all of this pain and hurt in his life? Bear in mind that no matter what he does in recovery, he still feels stalled. Why? See if you can find some clues in his story.

Jerry's Story

"I was born into a typical alcoholic home," Jerry said. "It was abusive, brutal, and crazy." As a younger child in this family, he said he was tormented a lot by his older brothers and sisters. Incredibly, he laughed as he told of one of his big brother's games called "Let's light Jerry on fire." Apparently this brother would chase him around the house or the yard throwing matches at him, which often set Jerry's clothes on fire! No adult was ever on hand to stop the attacks. Another recollection was of being at summer camp when his father died. When his mother came to bring him home, he was told that his father had died two weeks previously. Again, he told this story with a detachment that was downright eerie. *He didn't know that he was angry.* He didn't have any idea of what was causing the pain in his life and why he was stuck!

As a seven-year-old boy, Jerry recalled playing tag with a friend. Jerry was chasing the boy down the sidewalk when his friend ran out into the street and was hit by a truck. As a typical adult child, Jerry said, "But the rule in our house was, if you didn't talk about it, it didn't exist." So he tried to blot it out, act as if it never happened. There was no one in his family to help him understand this terrible event. There was no one he could talk to about it. He said his family kept telling him to forget it. They all behaved as if it had never happened. Now a forty-five-year-old man, Jerry was still reporting this event, looking for validation. "I saw him get hit by a truck, and I was chasing him." Well, think of the anger. Think of the grief. Think of the hurt.

If we don't accept the truth, we won't be able to make decisions about what is currently happening in our lives. As the saying goes, only the truth will set you free. Until we can accept reality, we do not have the truth to work with. Jerry's experiences were either worse or better than yours, but still, isn't his anger crystal clear? He was terribly angry! But until he could open up to that reality and all of the grief and sorrow that came along with it, he was not in control of that anger; it was in control of him.

Most people, to some degree, can relate to the concept of repressed anger. As deeply as the causes may be buried, they're hardly ever mysterious. If you have repressed anger, it's because you were hurt. It's because you felt victimized, or you felt discounted or demeaned, or you were not treated fairly. Your story may be very different from Jerry's, but until you can accept your reality, whatever that is, you're stuck with its negative power in your life.

Delusion and Denial

The opposite of acceptance is delusion and denial. If we will not accept the truth, then *the only thing we can do* is hide our reality with delusion and denial. And so our lives become full of shame, low self-esteem, victimization, and fear. Eventually, these conditions become the truth for us. When we accept our own reality, when we learn that whatever happened to us in the past *is* the truth, we will go beyond it and find freedom. So what is your truth? What caused the pain or even rage inside you? Coming up with that answer is far from easy. But if there's no understanding, progress is downright impossible.

What is your reality? Were you never really loved? Never held or hugged? The point of this questioning is not to look back and blame but to take back responsibility for the quality of your own life. Whatever that quality is from here on out is totally up to you. Without acceptance, there is only circular grief and sadness that lead to more of the same, not to healing. But when you put true acceptance in the mix, there may still be grief, but you can be healed from it. Once you have the truth—no matter how sad a truth it is—you can actually make a move to unhook the anchor rather than just make a longer chain.

Probably all of us have to make decisions about facing some hard truth about our families of origin. Sooner or later we have to decide what kind of contact we can reclaim and renew with our families. This decision must be made in spite of the fact that some family systems simply will not tolerate wellness because only sickness "fits." But even this realization, while painful, doesn't have to stop us in our tracks.

Dennis, for example, is a man who desperately wants to have a healthy, loving family—mother, father, and siblings. But his mother, father, and siblings are still consumed by abusive, alcoholic, insane behavior. And as sad as Dennis is that he didn't have the home life he always craved, he knows he can't go back. So of course he feels grief, but he is also healing. Since he understands his family dynamics—his truth—he can make the decisions that allow him to travel the path of wholeness and to get on with his own life.

Anger and Injustice

Many of the anger-fueled situations we face today were seeded in our past. "Anger work," if it is to be more than throwing logs on the fire, must enable us to understand both the nature of anger as it relates to us, and the anger-causing systems perpetuated by those early, learned patterns.

This work begins with a very clear definition of anger: *Anger is the emotional response to real or perceived injustice.* Whatever form it takes, anger is always about injustice. Whenever we did not receive what we thought was fair, just, or "should have been," we felt angry. To find the root of our anger, we need to look for the events of injustice in our past. Once we find them, we will see our anger spew forth like sparks from a smelter.

There are a lot of things that happened to us as children that can be described as gross unfairness. Being told we are stupid, ugly, that we will never amount to a damn, that we don't deserve to live; being denied compliments, acceptance, and affection are all crimes—and crimes by their very nature are unfair. Every crime has a victim, and every victim is the recipient of injustice.

Adult Children of Dysfunctional Families

Think about the recovery program, Adult Children of Dysfunctional Families. The very name says it all. The whole movement is about discovering that the sources of pain in adult life are often rooted in childhood experiences. Those of us who are children from dysfunctional homes are cheated out of our needs. It is unfair for children to witness drunkenness in a parent. And some dysfunctions that are not about chemical abuse are equally rank with injustice. Never winning approval no matter how hard we try or how successful we are is an affront to justice, as is being considered "less than" because of gender. All of it equals unfairness and all unfairness equals anger. The real question is never whether there is or is not anger, but rather how do we escape its clutches now and move down the yellow brick road toward forgiveness.

The Inner Child

Of all the familiar self-help terms, perhaps the one most loaded with poignant injustice is "inner child." In this context, of course, it always means *wounded* inner child. Who is more defenseless or deserving of acceptance and safety than a child? Inner child work focuses precisely on where the wound is and thus where the person is fixated as a child.

A frequent technique used in inner child work is to guide a group using a meditation to go back to the point of the injury. Slowly the leader quiets the group members, gently inviting them to travel back to their early childhood. "Sit quietly," they are told, "near the child that you were. Don't disturb. Don't interfere. Just look. What are you wearing? What are you doing? How do you feel? Who else is there with you? What has just happened?"

Many people cry as they remember. If there were such a thing as a pain meter in the room, it would blow up as people revisit their childhood injustices. When they remember those crushing, perhaps never to be remedied events, it hurts.

Such an exercise concludes with the participants writing letters to their wounded inner child. They tell their inner child what the child needs to hear. By doing this, they assert a truth that was denied them as children, and they rewrite the event with a different ending. Invariably, when such letters are shared, the messages have the same themes: "It really wasn't your fault"; "No one had a right to do that to you"; "You didn't deserve this"; "You are beautiful, lovely, and bright—no matter what anyone says"; "You have a right to be you, and you are more than okay just as you are"; "You have a right to laugh." This tragic litany catalogues every failure of the human family.

Talk about injustice! It is simply not fair that we were denied the normal affirmations and comforts that are the legitimate right of every human child. But they were denied us. And regardless of the particular circumstances, our response was anger—anger that has long been in need of healing.

Discovering More About Our Anger: An Exercise

The following exercise may be helpful to you in identifying both the origin and the "fingerprint" of anger that is still dirtying the clean lens of each new day. This exercise is a five-part discovery process that can most clearly be seen in the following five-column structure. To prepare for the exercise, write these column headings at the top of a clean sheet of paper:

Trait   Event   Injustice   Emotional Response   Face of Anger

Part One

To begin, review the following list of traits that are common to people in self-help groups. The idea is simply to rate yourself on a scale of one to ten as to how much each trait describes you. Next, write down the traits where you had high scores under the first column on your sheet. Don't be surprised if you have more than one high score. Most people do. The point of this exercise is to begin to personalize your anger.

Traits Indicating Anger (rate yourself from one to ten with one being low and ten being high):

1. Hypersensitivity

You tend to take things personally. You are often hypercritical, quickly imputing unfounded motives to others. You can take offense at the drop of a hat and can carry grudges interminably. One man, talking about a hypersensitive employee, said, "I told her I thought she looked nice today. Her immediate retort was, 'Are you saying I didn't look good yesterday?' "

2. Inflexibility

You can be a tyrant. When talking with others your attitude is, "I'll talk you down till you surrender." You feel you know everything, have no doubts, and insist on the last word on every topic. Your motto could be, "It's my way or the highway."

3. Fear of Rejection

You have a constant fear of "being found out." You shy away from events you may find enjoyable for fear others won't like you. Your first thought regarding any gathering is to avoid standing out in any noticeable way so you won't be shunted aside. Above all else you strive to "be nice."

4. Fear of Conflict

Even the hint of conflict is reason for you to run for cover. You will go to any lengths to avoid the slightest possibility of trouble with others. For you, experiencing conflict with someone in the past may have often caused this person to become enraged and then abusive in one form or another. This fear of conflict has invariably led you to many compromises of your integrity, so rather than assert yourself and risk inconveniencing another, you minimize your wants and needs, swallow your pride, and kiss your self-esteem good-bye.

5. Fear of Abandonment

Typical of anyone who has found that "closeness hurts," fear of abandonment is a malady of millions. For you, though, there is nothing you desire more than intimacy and yet there is also nothing you fear more. You have learned to expect betrayal. You expect to end up left behind and alone. And since expectation has a most uncanny way of fulfilling itself, more often than not you choose to depend on people who are not able to make a commitment. Thus the deadly cycle stays in place—again and again you are abandoned.

6. Fear of Disclosure

Self-revelation is just this side of jumping into an alligator pit for you. Although you may actively seek closeness, you find it nearly impossible to drop your mask and allow yourself to be known. You hide your feelings and inner self with all the passion of a miser protecting his or her gold. But your withholding of self doesn't give other people a real person to connect with.

7. Overachievement

Overachievers are relentlessly dogged by the shadow of failure. No matter how grand the achievement, it is never enough. Your great task in life is to *prove* yourself—perhaps to someone who may no longer be alive or could never be satisfied no matter what you accomplished. Your goal is to somehow fill up the bottomless dark hole in the middle of your core with success, success, and more success.

8. Control

You have a desperate need to influence outcomes. Because of this, you can never relax, go with the flow, let your guard down, or shake off the fleas of guilt. After all, if you are responsible and things are not perfect, who is there to blame but yourself? For this reason, you are always tired. It is hard work to be responsible for the whole world—or any part of it but yourself!

There are a great many other traits that could have been listed. This is not intended to be an exhaustive list. Its purpose is to illustrate the nature of anger and its invisible connection with who we are today. Can you relate to any of these traits? Place the traits that best describe you (the ones that scored the highest number) under the first column of your chart.

Part Two

Next, list an *event* that taught you to view and respond to your life in the way each of your traits describes. Anger-hooked people didn't fall out of trees fully formed at age thirty. We practiced. We were taught, and we learned. We learned from repeated events that taught us this is how it is. *This is life.* Injustice was experienced at the heart of those events, and *there* is the source of our anger. In each event is the wound that needs forgiveness and healing if we are ever to be free. When you remember what event is relative to each of the traits you have listed, write it down, tell how old you were, what happened, who was there, and what was said.

Here are some typical events recorded by others who have done this exercise:

Every Friday night I waited so hard for my father to come home and give me a hug that I pressed my nose against the window to watch for him. He never came. I never got that hug. My nose still hurts every time I feel lonely or afraid.

One event among many was when my father said to me (with the worst smirk in the world) when I told him I wanted to be a cheerleader, "Christ, Ellen, you can hardly walk let alone cheer. You'll embarrass the whole lot of us."

I remember we were pouring concrete for a chicken coop. I was about ten. My job was to mix the concrete in this big bucket with an old piece of wood lath. The lath broke. My father ran over and kicked me so hard in the rear end that my jaws slammed together and cut my tongue. I could *never* make a mistake—and everything I did was a mistake to him.

After my father died, my mother and I had to go live with my grandfather. His way of keeping me in line was to say that if I was bad he would take me to an orphanage. I lived in a constant state of fear. One day when I was about eight he got mad for some reason. He told me he was taking me to the institute and drove off with me shaking in the front seat. We went about fifty miles in silence before he said he'd give me another chance and turned around.

What were the events that caused the traits that you can recall? Where was the anger born in your life?

Part Three

Now write in the third column the *injustice* that was perpetrated on you for each event. What exactly was it that was not fair? Why were you hurt? This is usually not hard to figure out on an intellectual level, but it is emotionally very hurtful to pull this deeply buried material out into the light. Take all the time you need to think and then list the rights that were violated by these events.

Part Four

In the fourth column, list your emotional response to the injustice of each event. Strangely enough, anger is often *not* the first emotion people list. It may well be fear. It may be panic. The dominant emotional response may have been an overriding compulsion to please or hide or win or always, always to be correct. The upshot is that these feelings soon become habits and that habits, once they are formed, no longer need a reason to exist. They simply *are* because we have given them life by repeated reinforcement.

That's why, when we get down on ourselves because we feel frightened or angry, when "there is no reason for it," we are revealing that we don't understand the nature of conditional emotional response and the power of habit. *Of course* there is a reason we have these feelings. There is always a valid reason—even if it is forty or fifty years old. Habit knows no time limit. Then is now—unless we change it. And we cannot change anything we do not understand.

Part Five

In the last column on the chart, list a "face of anger" from the previous chapter. They are:

- Depression
- Smoldering Rage
- The Fidgets
- Secret Keeper
- Victim
- Switched Addictions

Given each trait, the event that caused it, and the resulting injustice and emotions, you will end up expressing anger in one face or another.

This exercise has been laid out horizontally because that's the way most of us think—straight across the page. In actuality, this model could be more accurately expressed in a circle, one effect flowing into another, each one tripping off the next. The more the face of anger is acted out, the more deeply entrenched the trait becomes. The more often the trait is repeated, the more often we create unjust events that trigger the same emotional response over and over again.

Think about the folk wisdom that says, "The child is parent to the adult." But is it not true that anger can also arise from a much more recent point of origin than our childhood? Of course. It not only can but almost certainly will. The reason is that what was begun in the past will continue to function in the present unless conscious, effective action is taken to alter its course. Systems beget systems. Relative to anger, the child is literally, as well as figuratively, parent to the adult.

Discovering More About Our Anger: A Second Exercise

This realization may be deepened by working out another version of the chart used in the first exercise. Make three column headings on a sheet of paper. Label the first one "Event." Then head the second column "Learned to Cope by . . ." The third column of the new chart can be headed "Repetition." For the first column, pick an event in your life that caused you pain, where an injustice occurred. Write it down. As a result of the event, did you learn to cope by trying harder or ceasing to try at all? By growing calluses or becoming hypersensitive? By becoming addicted to closeness or refusing to ever allow anybody to get close? Did you hide or did you act out to get noticed? As simple as this sounds, the true picture is not that easy to see. So take whatever time you need to come up with the actual coping mechanism you chose to deal with the injustice behind the event. Then write it down under the second column heading.

In the third column, list how you have continued to act out the coping techniques that may well have saved your life—if not your sanity—at an earlier age, but which now are no longer appropriate or healthy. Your chosen coping technique may once have been as comfortable as an old shoe. But a sharp nail has come poking through, and now that shoe can cripple you. If your coping technique was to become very passive and "nice," how are you still acting out that technique to your detriment? If your coping technique was to "finally show them, by God!" how is that hostility causing you harm today? What silly risks are you taking for no other reason than to retaliate for an event (which no doubt is a whole series of events) that happened to you twenty years ago? If your technique was to seek approval from others at all costs, what horrendous price has that extolled over the years? How many bad relationships have you endured? Think about the coping techniques that you used for each event and then write down the ways you are still using them today under the third column heading.

The origins of anger are not very mysterious once they're charted out. And the clearer they become, the less appealing they show themselves to be. Thus, the healthier we get, the less willing we are to put up with sickness—our own or others'. As our understanding of ourselves deepens, what needs to be done and why we need to do it begins to take shape. How could we attempt to get over a fear of dogs if we go on living with a dog that attacks us on a daily basis? First things first. We have to get rid of the savage dog. Yet even after we accomplish this, our habits remain. The damage remains. The necessity of addressing the wrongs done to us and then proceeding to forgiveness may be intellectually clear but emotionally confused. Many of us still hesitate. Faulty mental perceptions and fear often conspire to stop our journey to freedom. But we are truly stuck until we take action.

What Do We Now Know About Anger?

Two principles are at work here. Number one is simply that *you cannot dismantle anything you do not thoroughly understand*. Remember Charlie's difficulty with his garage door opener? Another telling example is a scene from a novel about terrorists who are planting a bomb in an airplane. As the scene begins, time is running out for the bomb disposal squad. The clock is ticking as they frantically try to figure out which wire to cut to disarm the bomb. If they cut the wrong wire, the bomb is sure to blow up in their faces. If they don't understand the mechanism well enough, they'll never be able to disarm it. In much the same way, all of our repressed anger and shame-based issues exist like little time bombs planted in our lives. If we don't understand them, we'll never know which wire to cut. Our hidden faces of anger and rage are always there and capable of blowing up. What a risk we run if we don't understand them!

The second principle is that *being a victim usually equals an unwillingness to take responsibility for our own lives*. If we habitually feel powerless, used, or that we're being "done unto," the problem may well be more with us than it is with them—no matter who *they* are. It can seem cruel to make this point too glibly or to people who are beaten down, people who are gravely hurt, or people who may not have the strengths or abilities or advantages that others are blessed with. But there are things we can do! Only we know the truth about ourselves. And even if taking responsibility for different areas of our lives isn't possible right now, we can take a moment to *think* about our situation. Recovery never requires the impossible. If confronting some difficulty head-on is too hard right now, we can cut it in half. If the situation that is causing the anger is too frightening for us to attack, we can still be willing to talk about it with a trusted friend. If we can't act on it, we can still say a prayer about it. We can at least read a book about it. Every one of those baby steps gets us ready to make the all-important decisions that will get us ready to make a move.

The fear and weakness we bring to a situation don't change the situation. They don't change our victim status even though we have a thousand reasons to excuse it. Excusing our own victimhood is irresponsible.

Perhaps you are in a situation where you are not being treated fairly at work. Because of your agreeable nature, you are always being asked to work overtime while other, less agreeable people are never asked. Have you gone in and complained? Have you talked straight? And if you have complained without getting relief, have you complained again? Have you really asserted yourself? Very often, when people are made victims, it's because they have not been assertive about their rights. Some of us who have experienced abusive relationships may have literally become *programmed* to tolerate abuse. We may resent the idea that personal responsibility is part of the solution. But if we see ourselves as victims and continually sense we are being taken advantage of, or if we find we are being abused over and over again in our lives, chances are we have been passive and unwilling to stand up for ourselves. In a real sense we set ourselves up to be victimized.

Empowerment through understanding. What rights do *you* have? What rights do you need to fight for? Is there someone you need to confront? It may be your kids, it may be your husband, it may be your wife, it may be a significant other. Whomever it may be, if you feel victimized, what do you need to say to that person?

Ten Defenses We Have Against Seeing the Truth

There are many common reasons or justifications that we use to avoid seeing the truth and, therefore, to avoid accepting the truth. But not accepting the truth makes us unable to make the decisions that will enable us to change our lives. Here's a list of ten familiar, human defensive refrains. Of course, these aren't the *only* ten, but they're a good starting place. As you consider each of these self-protective postures, it may be useful to rate yourself on a scale of one to ten, with one meaning, "This is not a problem, and I have never thought this way in my whole life," and ten meaning, "Yup, that's me. I can really relate to that."

Number one: I am not going to dig up this stuff because **I am not willing to sacrifice or to lose my whole life.** We often take this stance about a relationship that has become abusive or has just plain fizzled out. But if the relationship has gone on for a long time, the fear of aloneness may be so great that we think, "I am not going to uncover any terrible truths. I am going to hide behind delusion and denial and ignorance, because if I admit my true feelings, I'll have to give up everything I have, as flawed as it is. I'm simply not willing to sacrifice my whole life." But if you can relate to these thoughts, how much of a life do you already have? What is it that you are actually giving up? What is really so precious about the situation you are hanging on to? If there is abuse or a great deal of hurt in the relationship, speaking the truth about it doesn't make your situation any worse. It doesn't mean that you have given up your whole life. It means that you are getting yourself into a position where you can finally start creating and experiencing some happiness in life. It's exactly the opposite of having to give up anything.

Sometimes a situation is so painful that there is really no other choice but to speak the truth. Dan, for example, made his father's fondest wish come true by joining the family business. For much of his adult life Dan had buckled under to the domineering old man by pretending interest and enthusiasm for work he despised. For years he hung on, not facing the truth that this life-style was not for him. He refused to face the fact that his work was causing him depression, bleeding ulcers, and migraine headaches—because if he faced it, he would have to leave. And if he left, he would have to sacrifice his income, his status, and certainly his father's approval. He would have to sacrifice his whole career. He would have to start over from scratch in some junior position. His dilemma seemed so terribly unfair that he simply was not willing to act. Finally, a close friend made him look at his excuse. "What is it that you are really leaving?" the friend asked him. "Yes, you have a lot invested, *but what's it costing you to stay?* And if you *do* leave and start over, is it the end of the world? Will you really starve on the street?" The answer for Dan was that he wouldn't.

Risking security and facing a personal or professional relationship that is painful and unhealthy may well leave you in terrible financial straits. You may be terribly lonely and have low self-esteem as a result. But the hidden anchor can only hold you if you continue to believe your delusions and to deny your truth. How valuable is the source of so much pain? Will a positive decision really force you to give up everything? Maybe you won't have to give up as much as you imagine. Is hanging on worth the pain? Could the pain of change be any worse?

Number two: **It's not fair.** We say, "I refuse to deal with this issue because it simply isn't fair. I shouldn't have to cope with this mess that somebody else made. It just isn't fair!" Marcia, for example, fully expected to live into her old age with the husband she has made a home with for thirty years. Then one day he told her that he didn't want to be married anymore. Even worse, to add insult to injury, he admitted that there was another woman. The rage that Marcia feels is literally blinding. She simply cannot look at the facts of the situation. How understandable! Yet in spite of her legitimate resentment, Marcia is a victim of her own rage, unable to work with it in such a way that could truly release her from its painful paralysis. Sometimes even five, ten, or fifteen years down the road, those of us in Marcia's situation are still nursing and harboring that rage. Over time, that rage expresses itself in one or more of the faces of anger that permeates every part of our lives. And if we make no decision to change, then all of those years are wasted!

Unfairness is a fact of life. How we respond to that is up to us. Suppose a beloved spouse dies because he or she didn't take care of him- or herself. In some measure, this person was responsible for his own death. Perhaps he allowed himself to get one hundred pounds overweight. Or she smoked until she got emphysema or cancer and died many, many years before her time. The surviving spouse may be absolutely furious. *It is not fair that this happened.* Or suppose a child is killed by a drunk driver. *It is not fair.*

No one would disagree that some situations are hideously, stupefyingly unfair. *But they still have to be dealt with.* They have to be acknowledged and expressed. It is a good idea to write about situations we find ourselves in that are unfair. Writing our thoughts and feelings down often helps us to affirm and accept the fact that we are right: it is not fair. But until we can accept the unfairness of life, which doesn't mean we agree with it or approve of it, we cannot choose any other path. The hidden anchor, perhaps for the rest of our lives, will keep us fixated at the point where that pain happened. And that's not fair either.

Many severely mistreated adult children, when they start to recover, come face-to-face with real rage about what happened to them. "It's not fair that I was abused! It's just so unfair that I was passed from family to family because no one wanted me!" And of course it's true. All children deserve to be wanted and loved. They're right—what happened to them wasn't fair. But at some point, beyond validating the pain, they need to accept it and then go on—or the anchor will forever stay in place.

Are you hiding from some deep-seated anger because you resent the unfairness of what caused it? Can you see how we double the unfairness to ourselves when we use it as a hiding place? What price are we willing to pay for other people's crimes?

Number three: Another common excuse we use to stay anchored down is **I want revenge.** This posture is motivated by a powerful inner voice that says, "I'll show them! I'll make them eat their words, get down on their knees, and beg for my forgiveness!" Even years and years after we were wronged, that motivation may still direct the way we act. We can see it in our obsession to be successful or to always look good or to be in tight control. No matter what it costs, we'll show them! If you relate to this, write about it. You may surface plenty of evidence to justify this kind of obsessive behavior—which testifies to the strength of the hidden anchor—but whom are you hurting? Where is your revengeful attitude directed when you say, "I am absolutely not going to reconcile, forgive, or get on with my life because *they* don't deserve it." Obviously they may *not* deserve it. But who's paying the price if your desire for revenge keeps *your* anchor in place? Who loses?

Revenge can be a powerful issue. The mind will always move toward its predominant thought. If our predominant thought is of revenge, getting even, making other people grovel, our world can only be adversarial. That's the only direction our lives can take. Who then pays the price? The thought pattern we create is the only map we can follow. If we create a reality based on revenge, that stony ground is all we have to build on.

Who is the object of these revengeful feelings? Often the one who has inspired our fury is completely out of the picture. Sometimes they don't even know if we are still alive. Maybe they don't even know that we were slighted or injured. Perhaps they don't remember, and even if they do remember, how much of their time and energy do they spend in sorrow and regret over what they have done to us? Chances are, none. So who is paying the price for our hurt and anger? Who is being punished? And in the present day, who is the punisher? Revenge obsession is powerful. No matter what we do to try to achieve greater freedom, or greater recovery, until that anger is addressed, we are stuck.

Number four: **I am not going to make a decision to do anything because I am afraid.** What will happen if we make certain decisions? The sheer, naked fear can be terrible. Those of us who want to give up an addiction but are just so afraid of how a life based on abstinence will be often think, "How will I ever have fun again without alcohol? How can I possibly relax or feel good about myself?"

Fear of the unknown has many forms. "How will I feel better if I make this decision now? What will be left of my life if I give up my anger?" On some subtle level perhaps we may well know that validating a grudge has become the center of our lives. What will replace it if we give it up? Writing about it may make it fairly clear that something far superior is available to us. Once we do give the grudge up and move on, we will very likely look back and wonder what in the world we were waiting for.

Fear of what may come next keeps many of us absolutely rooted to where we are. It is good to remember that this fear is not always irrational. Some of the decisions we need to make may indeed risk physical danger. If we decide to leave a toxic, abusive relationship, for example, we may be putting our safety and perhaps even our children's safety in jeopardy. In these cases, careful planning and plenty of support are absolutely essential. But taking action is even more essential. If we allow the fear and the anxiety of moving on to be more powerful than the reward of moving on, then what are we condemning our lives to be? What quality of life can we hope for? If our lives are dismal and miserable, something has to be done. So, while it's understandable to be afraid of the uncertainty of the future if we make a change, choosing certain misery is hardly a rational option. Not to decide *is* to decide. If we won't decide to move on, we *are* deciding to continue to live with the consequences of what's happening in our lives right now. Nothing works better than fear to keep that anchor firmly in place.

Number five: **I choose to stay stuck in this bad place because I will not give up the dream.** Many of us have this fixation regarding a relationship. Even if the hoped-for reality is wildly impossible under the present circumstances, there are those of us who won't abandon our quest to be involved with another person because "I just don't want to give up the dream." But the fact may well be that if we are not willing to move on, we will never have anything *but* a dream. If the dream is of an ongoing, loving, spirit-filled, supportive relationship, and we are in a toxic, abusive, spiritless, hurtful relationship and we don't move on, we will never be in a position where our dreams can come true.

To stay in a bad place does not mean that somehow, some way, everything is going to be fine. It doesn't even mean that it won't get worse. What it means is that willful blindness is not the same thing as persevering idealism. Perhaps the dream itself doesn't have to be given up, but only our *version* of it. Perhaps the dream is not possible with this person—not because this person is bad, but because the relationship is not working. There may be no more hope for it. If you are stuck in a dream world, it may be helpful to get down the elements of your dream in black and white. On paper, what does your dream look like? Is it also your partner's dream? Is it reasonable or rational for you to cast other human beings, willing and able or not, into your own fantasies? Who is responsible for *your* dreams?

Number six: **I just can't.** While that statement covers a lot of ground, it may be true for some of us at the moment. Readiness to act takes time and work. If we're not ready to make the big decision to move on, can we begin by making some small decisions? If we cannot verbalize what we need to say to someone else, can we decide to say it aloud but only to ourselves? The only way to eat an elephant is one bite at a time. "Just can't" doesn't excuse total inaction. We may not be able to make a touchdown, but we can gain a yard if we want to. Perhaps we need to think about the injustice that caused our anger or take some action relative to a career, a relationship, or the way we parent our children. To flatly say, "I just can't" is at best a halftruth. If that's where you are, write out an honest answer to the question, *why can't I?* Some of the underlying reasons behind your paralysis may not seem insurmountable at all once they're down on paper. And even if there are compelling reasons to be cautious, *some* progress is always possible.

Number seven: **I can't do this work because I cannot hurt the other person.** "I just can't say the truth because it will hurt my loved one's feelings. This decision is unthinkable because my loved one would be devastated." Many times when we say these things, what we are really saying is we can't bear to hurt *ourselves*. Our inner dialogue says, "It's terribly dangerous to hurt other people's feelings because if I do, they will turn around and hurt me. They might say cruel things to me. They could get angry and make me feel guilty. They won't think I'm a good person." Those of us who have been programmed to avoid hurting other people at any cost are absolutely paranoid about doing the wrong thing, about being rejected, about being made to feel guilty. Well, how great a crime can it be to speak our own truth? The important thing is to check our motives. If we are not willing to risk a change for the better, we have to ask ourselves *why not?* If our answer is, "Because I cannot hurt someone else," check that out. Is it really that we don't want that person to hurt us?

Genuine consideration of other people requires courageous honesty. But how often do we hurt other people by *not* telling the truth? Many times in relationships we absolutely wear down the other person through our indifference, through our emotional withdrawal, through our constant, cold hostility. We strike out in these passive ways because we are trapped in a situation we do not want to be in. Remember that being a victim is about being unwilling to take responsibility for our own lives. If we're already treating our partners with negativity and indifference, is that not painful to them? The issue is not about hurting them or not hurting them, or even about pain or no pain. *Both ways hurt*. The issue is, which way must we go that will eventually lead to freedom? It doesn't make sense to choose an option that hurts *and only leads to more pain*. To speak the truth can hurt a lot, but it doesn't lead to more pain. It may take time to get ready to speak out, but let it take time. If we're coming to the point where we can actually share our truth, even though that hurts, we're truly gaining freedom.

Many people in recovery have gone to the brink thinking they could never do it, have it, or be it—whatever "it" is. It may mean leaving a job and finding a new career. It may mean adopting a child. Making a mighty leap doesn't always mean ending something. It may very well mean starting something that we need to do. But once we've made that leap, then we can look back and say, "How could I not have done this sooner?" The benefit that comes from these changes is enormous. It doesn't mean that we won't hurt others. But we've gone from death to life, not just from death to more death. So if you are staying anchored in indecision because you can't hurt someone else, think long and hard about it.

Write about it so you can uncover what you are really telling yourself.

Number eight: **If I make a change, someone will be mad at me.** Maybe someone will. But how fearful should we allow ourselves to be of someone else's anger? Unless we're dealing with a real threat of violence—and some of us are—it won't kill us to provoke a little anger. It's true that when we get honest and make a decision to change, somebody may get mad at us. But so what? Often what is behind our fear of provoking anger is our desperate need for universal approval. We have learned that if people get mad at us, they will reject us, so we try to get approval from everyone. But we *don't need* to get approval from everyone. We can survive and flourish even if the people we love best get angry at us and reject us. We may have to live with that rejection for a while, but to simply stop based on that reason, the myth that we cannot get anyone angry at us is like shooting ourselves in the foot and then joining a running race.

Number nine: **I can't go forward because I don't know how.** "I would like to make a decision and move toward a change, but I don't know how. I'm confused. I don't know what to do." Pretended or exaggerated ignorance can be a terrible stumbling block. And sometimes we are literally too tired to think. But we can always get a toehold on the truth if we want it enough. We can be humble enough to get some support and make a modest start. If we do not avail ourselves of an effective support system, the odds are against us. But if we will go out and find them, there are wonderful people to talk to, informative books to read, and seminars and workshops galore. If we would really like to move on but don't know how to, we can learn. Not knowing is not a reason for indecision.

Number ten: **Any big change is impossible for me because God says I can't.** "God says I can't make people angry. God says I can't be selfish, meaning doing something for myself. God says I can't leave a relationship." If this is your predicament, try writing out an answer to these crucial questions: Who is your God? Is God, as you understand God to be, someone who wants you to wither away in an abusive, dangerous relationship?

One woman went back to her physically abusive husband because someone convinced her that God demanded that she do so. As it happened, this woman came within an inch of being murdered. Is this the desire of God, as you understand God to be? Of course no one can tell us who our God is. But if we think, "Yes, God wants me to put myself in a position where I don't want to be, where every instinct I have tells me to get away, where staying endangers me or my children," we need to think about that long and hard. Is that really *God* talking? Is that the message of a loving God? The point, of course, is not for us to remake God in the way that we would like God to be. If you do think of God this way, would you be willing to check out your understanding of God with some other good people? Would you be willing to go to a group and find people you think have some real serenity and peace of mind? Would you ask them to share with you *their* God, as they understand God to be? There are at least a few truly wise people in nearly every group. Use them as a sounding board if you believe that God doesn't want you to deal with the causes of your anger. Misperceptions about God can and do cause a lot of unnecessary grief.

Now go back over these ten reasons that we all use to stay stuck. These sticking places are the false myths that create our boundaries, which are the borders, walls, or limited spaces that we live within. Write down the reason or reasons you are using to stay stuck, and then ask yourself, "What boundary have I created here?" If you are stuck because of revenge, for example, what boundaries does that set up in your life? Is there any peaceful place within the lines you've drawn, or is there nothing but hostility? If you believe that God says you "can't," then what boundary have you created around God, as you understand God to be? Will you never get close to a God who truly cares about and loves you?

Before going on, take some time to write about whatever myth seems to fit you. Personalize that myth so that you can better understand the boundaries that you have established for yourself. Remember that understanding leads to power, and this power enables us to make better choices in our lives.

3 ✿ ✿ ✿

Resentments—Growing Up in a Dysfunctional or Alcoholic Family

Our resentments determine where our boundaries are because our mind-set dictates our reality. Think about how powerful our mind-set, or our habitual way of looking at things, really is. Our definitions of life, of the world, of who we are, are all part of the mind-set that dictates our reality. If we are filled with resentment, a big portion of our lives is held captive by that anger and that resentment. And the truly frightening part is, there are a lot of people, especially we adult children, with anger so horrendous that it sparks out of our eyes and ears, but we often *don't even know we're angry*. That galling knot in our stomachs has become so habitual that we aren't even aware of our need for forgiveness and reconciliation. But if the damage that caused that resentment is not brought up to the conscious level where we can truly see it and understand it, it absolutely controls our lives. That angry mind-set and resentful perception of life are where our expectations come from. They're where our boundaries come from. They're what dictates the quality of our lives.

If we are harboring a great deal of anger and resentment, *we* may not be aware of it, but others almost surely are. Chronic anger is highly visible. And nearly everyone we meet in life is going to respond to us according to what they see. Very, very few people have the sensitivity or even the interest to look beyond the outer appearance of other people's angry, resentful attitudes. In this very real sense, the resentments we carry with us define our relationships with other people. If we are full of anger and resentment, it shows in our face; it shows in our body language; it shows in the tone of our voice; it shows in the way that we talk to people, even if the words we use are not hostile and angry. It only follows that people are going to respond to whatever it is we show them. If what they see is negative, negativity will likely be what we get back.

Dysfunctional Families

What's at the root of our resentments about our families? First, we need a definition of *dysfunctional families*. Many of us resist the idea of calling our families dysfunctional. Some of us insist that our families were entirely and thoroughly toxic in every way. But isn't it true that *everyone* had problems in their families? Surely the difference is a matter of degree. Some families are much healthier than others. Yet there are no perfect people on this planet, so how could there be a perfect family? The point is not to label some families as sick and others as healthy, but to take a less judgmental look at the messages, the patterns, and the mind-sets that we absorbed from them. If 95 percent of those messages were healthy and positive and spiritual, then how lucky we are! Let's work on the 5 percent that weren't. But people who grew up in severely dysfunctional families don't have the benefit of 95 percent healthy input. They may have received only 5 percent or 3 percent of what they needed. But in any case, everybody comes from an imperfect family.

In our dysfunctional family system, our love seemed to be wasted because it didn't get us what we wanted and needed. The reciprocal love we were looking for wasn't really attainable from those we "wasted" our love on. In a real sense, love can only exist when it is active from both sides. In our families, our love didn't work. *But the fact is that attainable love is the right and primary need of every human being.* If we didn't get that love or acceptance or sense of self-worth, we were indeed cheated and damaged. We had a right to something we never got. So naturally we're angry about being denied our rightful share of love from our families! As *Anger is always the emotional response to injustice.*

The stories told at adult child meetings illustrate every kind of heartrending injustice. The little girl waiting for her father to come home with her nose pressed against the window night after night. The shame-filled son of two alcoholics who told of hiding in the backseat of his parents' car, terrified that his friends would see him. It's simply not fair for people to live that way.

Adult children of dysfunctional or alcoholic families, regardless of how they label themselves, have core anger issues. Recovery or spiritual freedom to a large extent depends upon dealing with those anger issues. It is not enough to simply acknowledge that we were hurt and that we are angry about it. Admission is a critical beginning, but that in itself is not sufficient. Recovery means dealing with and rising above anger.

Resentments

Resentment is a combination of the emotions and actions and thought patterns resulting from our unresolved anger at an injustice. Resentment comes from anger just as smoke comes from fire. If we can say that there was injustice in our lives and that it hurt, then we are also likely to be resentful. This is a key admission because living with chronic resentment is like trying to run a race with one foot tied to a stake. If one foot can't move, how are we going to run? And if that race is so important that the outcome will dictate the quality of our lives, then we are faced with a real dilemma. The whole point is to untie our foot from the stake.

It's important to *personalize* your resentments so they are real to you. Exactly how were you victimized in your particular family? What was unfair? Specifically, how were you cheated? What was the injustice done to you? When you didn't get what you needed, how did you feel? What was it that you needed and didn't get? Many adult children sum it up by saying, "All I ever wanted was to be loved. Yet no matter how hard I worked, no matter how many points I made in the basketball game, no matter how well I took over running the house—no matter what—it was never there. And all I ever wanted was to be loved."

Writing Down the Injustice: An Exercise

In your particular family what was the injustice? It often helps to write out these facts and feelings. Think as clearly and as specifically as you can and describe the pain you suffered. Once you get it down on paper, the depth of the injustice that created your anger and then your resentment becomes pretty clear. Next ask yourself how those early "lessons" still influence your life today and write these down. If you were never picked up and hugged, for example, the lesson you may have learned was that you are not lovable. If you were constantly told to shut up or go away, you may have learned that your feelings don't count. If you heard, "What did I ever do to deserve a child like you?" or "Why can't you be nice like your brother?" a thousand times a day, chances are you learned there was something basically wrong with you. Are you still reacting to those lessons?

As you reread your own account of where and how you got cheated, you can get beyond just measuring the resentment. You can come to a deeper understanding of the cause and the source of that resentment. Understanding goes beyond deciding whether or not you have a right to be angry. No one can tell you that you don't have that right. No one can talk you out of your legitimate anger. You may have every reason in the world to justify your resentment. But regardless of the reason, if you are carrying that resentment around, you are the one who is paying for it. That's really the issue. What price are you willing to pay for carrying this resentment around?

Resentments fixate us at the point of our pain. If we will not rise above our resentments, then we must *again* bear the trauma of the injustice that we suffered long ago. It becomes a double tragedy. It's bad enough that some painful situations hurt us ten, twenty, thirty years ago and that we were never loved. It's bad enough that they happened then, but if we lug around the resentments these situations caused, they hurt us *again every day of our lives.* In those of us who have very deeply ingrained resentments, these decades-old circumstances haunt every hour of every day. Literally, not an hour goes by that's not darkened and soured by the anger and the resentments we are still living out.

But then was then and now is now. Back then we didn't have a choice. Back then we had no power to stop the abuse that created the anger and the resentments in our lives. But now we do. We have the power of understanding, and it is up to us to decide if we are going to continue living under the bondage of these old resentments and these old angers. We can overcome and change that if we choose—through forgiveness and reconciliation.

Boundaries

Uncontested resentments make it impossible for us to establish and live within healthy boundaries. This is a critical point. Many of us adult children of dysfunctional or alcoholic families have read or gone to meetings or heard speakers talk about *boundaries*. It can be said that all adult children issues are about bad boundaries. Our rights are a good example. Many of us don't have healthy boundaries regarding our rights.

What are our rights? How many rights do we have? Where do our rights end and another person's begin? Often we have terrible boundaries regarding intimacy. What is love? How much is it safe to trust? Who is safe to trust? Is it ever safe to believe that we are part of a healthy, loving relationship? The answers to these questions are dictated by our boundaries.

Adult children typically have very fuzzy boundaries in regard to success and happiness. How much is enough? It may be that we have no idea of how much is enough. Perhaps, for us, there are never enough things: there is never enough work; there is never enough success; there is never enough money. Or maybe it went exactly the opposite way. Perhaps the message we internalized is that we don't deserve *anything*. We don't deserve any happiness. We don't deserve any prosperity. We don't deserve any success. Either extreme shuts us out of the good stuff in life.

As long as we harbor uncontested resentments, we won't have healthy boundaries. Healthy boundaries simply cannot be set around what we don't feel entitled to. That's the principle. Boundaries are about entitlement. What do you feel you are entitled to? If you feel you are not entitled to love or your own feelings or prosperity, something in you won't let you have them. If you feel you are not entitled to your own rights or to say no, then you will inevitably give away your rights and say yes.

Now let's take a graphic look at this issue of entitlement and healthy boundaries. The point is to get clear about our uncontested resentments, because these are the "bad boundary" areas that deny us healthy entitlement.

The Resentment Chart

What injustice did I experience?	What boundaries and rights did this injustice effect?	How do these bad boundaries influence my life today?
1. *Universal Criticism*	the right to feel good about myself; the right to take risks	perfectionism, procrastination, settling for second best
2. *Sibling Comparison*	the right to be valued for who I am; self-esteem	unhealthy relationships, materialism, inappropriate competitiveness
3. *Emotional Unavailability of Parents*	disbelief in true intimacy; the right to trust; the right to feel safe	dependent relationships, superficiality, self-sabotage
4. *Feelings Were Discounted*	distrust; ignorance of and self-destruction of feelings	emotional flatness, pretended emotion, sense of estrangement
5. *Abusive Touch*	disbelief in personal safety; the right to expect safe touch	abusiveness to others, emotional withdrawal, sexual frigidity

What injustice did I experience?	What boundaries and rights did this injustice effect?	How do these bad boundaries influence my life today?
6. *No Touch*	disbelief in true intimacy; the right to comfortably touch and be touched	fear of commitment, dependence in relationships
7. *Body Shame*	self-acceptance; the right to be flawed	obsessive about appearance, excessive fear of aging
8. *Repeated, Shameful Behavior on the Part of Parents*	the right to belong; distrust of authority	grandiosity, feeling "other side of the tracks," chronic distrust and insecurity
9. *Always Expected to Know But Never Given Time to Learn*	the right to make a mistake; the right to try new things without being punished	pretended ignorance, perfectionism, sense of inferiority
10. *Learned Acceptance Was Conditioned on* _____	the right to be imperfect; the right to refuse; the right to be tired	hyper-responsibility, denial of pain, people-pleasing

This Resentment Chart lists ten extremely common situations that teach shame to adult children. Remember that there is injustice at the heart of these situations, and injustice creates the anger that creates resentment. The focus here is that these resentments translate into bad boundaries. These ten don't make up an exhaustive list. You may come up with other situations that are more appropriate for you. As you think these through, it will be hard not to see that resentment is at the heart of the bad boundaries that cause later problems in your life.

Ten Situations that Teach Shame

Number one is **universal criticism.** If you were brought up with universal criticism, nothing you did was ever done well enough. No matter how successful you were, no matter how well you tried to clean the house, it was never clean enough. The people whose opinion mattered to you never gave you credit.

Now look at the middle column of the Resentment Chart. What boundary issues might arise for someone who has been bombarded with this criticism? Remember that you cannot have healthy boundaries around what you feel you are not entitled to. If you were formed and shaped by universal criticism, would you feel you are entitled to be satisfied with your accomplishments? Would you feel that you had a right to be proud of your accomplishments? Would you feel entitled to take a risk or to try something new? Almost certainly not. You learned that to try is to fail. If you give your all and your all is too little, you automatically lose. Who wants to be a loser and to be set up for all that abuse? So you feel you don't have a right to try new things or to take a risk or to feel satisfaction about your accomplishments.

Now, look at how these things are influencing your life today, the third column. The answer is fairly obvious. If you have lived with universal criticism and developed bad boundaries around how much is enough or how good is good enough, you may act out as a perfectionist or a procrastinator. You will often sabotage your success because success involves risk. Success means being willing to try new things, to find out where new possibilities are. But if you lived with the feeling that you don't have a right to succeed, chances are you won't try. You may act out by settling for second best and telling yourself you are happy about it. Of course you have resentment about that. And if you don't deal with the resentment so you can begin to establish healthy boundaries, what are the chances that you will ever act differently?

Number two is **sibling comparison.** Adult children often grow up with unflattering sibling comparison. "Why can't you be as smart as your sister?" "Why can't you be as handsome as your brother?" Perhaps you were often told with a sigh, "Your sister was never any trouble to us," the implication being that you were an absolute pain in the neck. Or perhaps you were compared with a cousin or a neighbor who always got better grades or was more popular in school. Very possibly you learned to think you didn't have a right to feel okay about who *you* were. You didn't know you had the right to feel whole and complete, let alone special.

Now if you don't feel entitled to feel unique or special, how might you act that out? One of many ways is the manner in which you strive for intimacy. Perhaps you will get into unhealthy relationships, because you feel you don't deserve anything better, that you don't deserve to be loved. Or perhaps you will become materialistic, showing the world how unique and special you are by how many things you have. You might think of this as *peace through acquisition.* You reason that the things you have will make up for all that withheld acceptance, wasted love, or crushing sibling comparison. But, of course, it never does. That's the problem with this kind of compensatory approach. It is a lie. It doesn't make up for what wasn't there. Is it any wonder where the bad boundaries come from?

Number three is **emotional unavailability of parents**. Your parents may have been physically present but emotionally unavailable. Where would the bad boundaries be set in this situation? What might you feel you don't have a right to? You might decide that you cannot trust anyone. You may have learned that it's dangerous to be vulnerable, so you grew up never wanting to take a personal risk. Your feelings simply weren't safe. How might you act that out?

One possibility is in dependent relationships. In trying to compensate for your lack of emotional connection with your parents, you might give all of your power away in relationships. You may be willing to endure any amount of abuse if only someone is there. This is a demonstration of bad boundaries. Or you may wind up trusting no one. With fear of vulnerability and commitment, you may never allow yourself to get into a relationship of any depth. Or you sabotage it if you accidentally do get into such a relationship. Why? Because you don't feel you have a right to an equitable partnership because of your earlier experience of emotional deprivation. Resentment? Absolutely. It isn't fair.

Number four is that your **feelings were discounted.** In one way or another, you learned that your feelings don't count. Maybe you were told that you shouldn't feel anger or fear, or that you don't have a right to feel proud of yourself. You learned it wasn't strong or nice or safe to have feelings. Perhaps you heard, "If you think that hurts, I'll give you something to cry about!" This message told you that your pain wasn't real or important. Where might you have boundary issues? Like almost all adult children, you may have a deep distrust of your own feelings. You may pretend to have feelings that aren't there. You may not know what your feelings are. And you may not even *have* feelings. Perhaps you literally killed them, because your feelings set you up for so much pain. Since you learned that your feelings didn't count anyway, you simply refused to have them.

Now how might you act out if you don't trust your own feelings? Where would the poor boundaries be? Not surprisingly, you may stuff your feelings. Chances are you might look around to see how other people are emotionally reacting so you can take your cue from them, not from your own heart. If your feelings were discounted, you may have trouble just getting along with people because you don't let people know who the real you is. You won't show them. Maybe you do this because you're afraid, but just as likely it may be because *you don't know* who the real you is. How could you not have resentment? It wasn't fair that you grew up in an environment where your feelings were discounted.

Number five is **abusive touch.** Abusive touch, including everything from incest to being slapped, pinched, or cruelly tickled, is a common source of long-standing resentment. If you lived with abusive touch, what boundary issues would arise for you? Perhaps you internalized that you don't have a right to physical touch, period. You learned that touch is not safe. Intimacy is another boundary issue commonly affected by abusive touch. Most intimacy includes touching, and it doesn't have to be romantic or sexual. With people who are important to us, touch is a beautiful language that communicates very deeply and meaningfully. If you grew up with abusive touch, however, you may be incapable of comfortably touching anyone. You may even have trouble with a hug or a pat on the shoulder. Just putting your arm around someone may be a strain. This is a boundary issue. Somewhere you learned that touch is dangerous and should be avoided.

How might you act that out? You may be a perpetrator of abusive touch yourself. This is just as much a boundary issue as shrinking from touch. You may have no real sense of rights—yours or anybody's. If this is the case for you, professional counseling is indicated. There are many people ready and able to help you.

Perhaps you think of yourself as too "intellectual" for emotional expression. Perhaps you've become stereotypically frigid, whether you are male or female. You may very well have deep and true feelings inside, but there is no way to express them because you learned touch is not safe.

Number six is **no touch.** Many, many adult children have touch issues because they never were touched. Indifference is also abuse. To never be held, to never be hugged, to never be touched can be as abusive as getting slapped in the face. If you didn't experience touch, where might your boundary issues be? It's likely that you don't feel a right to ask for touch, which means that you don't feel the right to ask for what you need. In a relationship, for example, you may not believe you have the right to ask for commitment. Or perhaps your touch denial translates into fear of abandonment, where you become so obsessive about and possessive of the other person that you spend every waking hour trying to get enough touch to make up for the past. But of course, the problem is that there is not enough touch in the world to make up for that. Your touch hunger can drive people away.

How might that dilemma be acted out? How might you behave if you feel you don't have a right to a commitment or to ask for what you need? Or if you're on the other side, and so expect everyone you meet to fill up your emptiness? Responses you may have include abusive relationships, fear of commitment, running away from relationships, confusing need with love so that there can only be weak, dependent relationships. Talk about resentments! Over time they may become so habitual, you don't even know they are there.

Number seven is **body shame.** Perhaps because of the size of your ears or nose or whatever, you were absolutely humiliated about your body, about the way you looked. Maybe you were overweight or maybe you were thin, but you were constantly made aware of your flaw and hounded about it. What rights might that endanger? If you grew up with body shame and a feeling of embarrassment about how you looked, you probably feel you don't have a right to be imperfect or flawed. You don't know you have the right to be who you are, to feel good about yourself. The sense of injustice generated by body shame is powerful.

How might you act that out? You may become obsessive about the way you look. You may do hours of aerobics each day or get enough plastic surgery to support an insurance company. And all for what? To make up for the torment and teasing and pain of the past. You may be trying to make your body "good enough," but the question is, good enough for whom? Who are you still trying to impress? It's all living in the past.

Maybe because of this body shame, you have never been able to accept a compliment or to experience contentment in who you are. Just the inevitability of getting older may be a great trauma for you. Accepting your body is a matter of healthy boundaries. Until you realize that *you* are not just your body, that there is a person of value there, you will be resentful. But that resentment will come out sideways in many different directions.

Number eight is **repeated, shameful behavior on the part of parents.** Some of us, every Saturday night, had to go find our parents and drag them home from the bars. Some of our mothers often had "uncles" over to spend the night. We may have been so young that we didn't exactly know what all that was about, but we knew these men weren't relatives and that something wasn't right about this. There are many more examples of shameful behavior on the part of parents.

Dysfunction, of course, comes in degrees.

But there are a lot of adult children—more than anybody realizes—who were burdened with their parents' shameful behavior to a *great* degree. Maybe they had all the love in the world for their parents or parent, but even so, they constantly witnessed parental behavior that made them cringe. If that is what you grew up with, which of your rights became boundary problems? You may feel, for example, that you don't have a right to a real "home." You may feel you don't have a right to belong anywhere. Perhaps it's not safe for you to trust authority. You might act out those beliefs in any number of ways. You may act them out in the form of grandiosity. If your parents were unacceptable, you'll make a point of showing the world how worthwhile you are. You may be so sure you won't be granted respect that you'll try to *buy* it. In effect, you try to substitute materialism for pride.

You may never be able to sense that someone else cares about you. You may constantly be under painful stress, because no matter how much love comes to you from husband, wife, kids, friends, you can't believe that it's true. You can't trust them or find security or serenity in the fact that they are there for you and will not leave. No matter how reliable your loved ones are, you believe that you will be hurt, disappointed, or that things won't work out. Who wouldn't have resentments over that?

Number nine is you were **always expected to know but never given time to learn.** This is a common adult child reality. Perhaps you were expected to know how to cook a family dinner or make a bed perfectly at age seven. Maybe someone thought you should know how to hit a home run, but you were never given time to learn. Maybe every time you didn't perform perfectly, you experienced some kind of punishment, either verbal or nonverbal. Perhaps you were actually hit or maybe you were put down or called names. If that is what you grew up with, what rights did you learn you were not entitled to?

For starters, you weren't entitled to make a mistake. You couldn't try new things without being hurt, punished, or abused. You were not entitled to be yourself. So how might that lack of entitlement get acted out? You may play the dummy. By pretending you don't understand, you can't be held responsible for making a mistake. Another way is to be a perfectionist. Early on you may decide that if you are going to be punished for making a mistake, you simply will never make a mistake. That means you have to always be the best, come in first, get only straight *A*'s on your report cards. If you ever come in second or get a *B*, you feel like a failure. Your self-esteem is shaken.

Why such an extreme reaction? It is another boundary issue around not feeling entitled to make a mistake—which is, of course, what it means to be human. Who wouldn't resent the expectation of being superhuman?

Number ten is you **learned that acceptance was conditioned on** _____. Was your acceptance and approval and sense of okayness granted not because of who you are, but only on some condition? What word fills in the blank for you? Work? Were you only accepted relative to how hard you could work or how much you could produce? Did you get approved of and affirmed only by being super-responsible? Maybe you became a perfect little mother at age ten or the man of the house at age nine. Maybe your acceptance was conditioned on how tough you were. Never admitting you were hurt. Never admitting there was anything you couldn't do. If this was the message, then what do you think you are not entitled to? Certainly not to say, "ouch." Nor do you think you can say, "No, I don't want to," "It costs too much," "It hurts too much," or "I'm not going to do that." Therefore, you have terrible boundaries around those issues.

Another example that is very common for a lot of adult children, especially women, is acceptance based upon being "nice." Nice girls don't say so. Nice girls don't ask for what they want and need—they think about others' needs instead. If that's what you learned, what don't you have a right to? What are you not entitled to? You are surely not entitled to say, "Get the hell away from me. You are stealing my cookies, and you don't have a right to steal my cookies." You've been taught that nice girls give their cookies away at the fourth-grade party. But the truth is, they don't; passive people do. The point is that boundaries will always be formed around our sense of entitlement.

As a final example, your acceptance may also hinge on always being right. Perhaps your most successful attempts to get acceptance depended on your always having something to say. Maybe you became a smart aleck and a showoff in your pursuit of approval and love. No matter how you fill in the "condition" blank for yourself, what you write there will be what you had to do to get validated and affirmed. But chances are, adequate, meaningful acceptance and approval was not there to be had no matter how hard you worked, no matter how responsible you were, no matter how tough, or nice, or "right" you were.

As a result of these conditions, what do you feel you are not entitled to? If you work compulsively, perhaps you do not feel entitled to take time off for leisure or recreation. If you are always responsible, you may not think you are entitled to much either. You may not feel you have permission to say, "This isn't my problem; it is yours. You take care of it." You have to be responsible for all people at all times. As a result, you have terrible boundaries.

If you are locked into being "nice," you probably don't think you should stand up for yourself if it is inconvenient for someone else, even if it needs to be said. And if you feel you have to be right at all times, you probably don't think you can afford to be ignorant about anything. What a heavy burden to carry around!

How might we act out our resentment about all ten of these injustices? Our compulsive behaviors answer this question loud and clear. To understand the dynamic beneath all of this, we need to become quite clear about where the injustice is, which creates the anger, which creates the resentment. Confronting our resentments gets the major obstacle out of the way so that we can begin to set healthy boundaries. Only then can real healing and spiritual growth begin to take place in our lives.

4 ✚ ✚ ✚

Forgiveness

What does *forgiveness* really mean? We know it's desirable and important, but what is it all about? First of all, forgiveness is a *spiritual* phenomenon. The spiritual dimension comes ahead of all else because it's totally possible to know and understand every rational aspect of forgiveness and still not be able to do it. Knowing isn't the same as doing. Readiness to forgive involves switching gears to a more emotional, meditative frame of mind. The goal is to get *beyond* our minds to the wider, deeper awareness that is spiritual understanding. Forgiveness is more than just the act of forgiving. Ordinarily, when we think about forgiveness, we automatically picture someone we're terrible angry at whom we need to let off the hook. Forgiveness is seen as an act of will or a deed of some kind. But simply trying to work up the juice to cancel an old debt is not the first step. First there is a state of mind.

The Forgiving State of Mind

The mentality of forgiveness comes *before* the act. If we become so consumed with the injustice we've suffered, then that part of our lives, which includes the hurt, the anger, the grief, and the sadness, becomes the whole. But that one piece, no matter how grievous, is no more than a part; it doesn't have to be the whole. The mind-set of forgiveness is created in people who have been able to grow beyond their painful, sad, hurting situations. Even when they suffer for years, they know that suffering isn't all of life. They see the hurting part within the context of a much larger whole, and they see the whole of life as primarily benevolent, primarily good.

"You know what I finally came to understand?" a man in a self-help group shared. "The world is much friendlier than I am. The truth is that the world is friendlier toward me than I am toward the world." This mentality, he was discovering, was giving him an extremely difficult time forgiving anyone else. A negative, cranky, hostile, victim mentality toward ourselves in particular, and life in general, makes it almost impossible for us to forgive others. The wider context that promotes or prevents forgiveness has to do with our basic attitude about openness and friendliness. What is your basic attitude toward the presence of beauty in the world? What is your basic attitude about other people? Are they allies or friends you haven't met yet, or are they automatically cast as the enemy? Do you always feel afraid of new people because they are likely to hurt you? These attitudes form the underlying framework of all our thinking.

A poem titled "Renascence" by Edna St. Vincent Millay draws a vivid, memorable picture of just this attitudinal framework, this context. The poem is about a woman who got so discouraged with life that she wanted to die. She was so full of frustration, hurt, and grief (and, in our terminology, shame) that it all got to be too much. She wished for death. So in the magic that poetry allows, this person died. She saw herself sink beneath the earth into a grave. For a while she was relieved and happy. Nobody was hurting her. She didn't have to put up with stress. She didn't have to endure unfairness or cruelty or inconvenience. Nobody was giving her a raw deal or even a dirty look. She was peacefully alone, and she liked it.

But after a while she began to miss being alive. She began to remember the beauty of life. She began to long for all of those things that she never valued in the first place because she was in a habitual state of shame. She wanted another crack at life. So she started to cry out. She had a "conversion experience," some would say. Or she "took a First Step" you might say if you are a Twelve Step person. She decided she wanted to live again because her withdrawal had cost her too much. Now she wanted to breathe the sweet air. She wanted to see a sunset. She wanted to see a bird fly. She was reaching the state from which forgiveness comes.

Having changed her mind, she prayed, she begged, she called out. And so she was resurrected—which is another word for forgiveness and reconciliation. In answer to her prayers, a great thunderstorm came, and she was washed up from the grave. With the thought that resentment and hostility are death, and that reconciliation with the wholeness of life is rebirth, listen to the beautiful, poetic language describing her dilemma.

> Oh God, I cried, give me new birth
> And put me back upon earth!
> Upset each cloud's gigantic gourd
> And let the heavy rain, downpoured
> In one big torrent, set me free,
> Washing my grave away from me!

What was she doing but begging for the power of forgiveness, the power of reconciliation? So she was resurrected. And how did she feel when she looked around and realized she had another chance for freedom and happiness?

> About the trees my arms I wound;
> Like one gone mad I hugged the ground;
> I raised my quivering arms on high;
> I laughed and laughed into the sky,
> Till at my throat a strangling sob
> Caught fiercely, and a great heartthrob
> Sent instant tears into my eyes;
> O God, I cried, no dark disguise
> Can e'er hereafter hide from me
> Thy radiant identity!
> Thou canst not move across the grass
> But my quick eyes will see Thee pass,
> Nor speak, however silently,
> But my hushed voice will answer Thee.
> I know the path that tells Thy way
> Through the cool eve of every day;
> God, I can push the grass apart
> And lay my finger on Thy heart.

This is the mind-set from which forgiveness comes. It is much more than just an intellectual or verbal act of forgiving someone. So often at meetings people will say, "I forgive, but I will never forget." Well, what does that mean? Does it mean that they are willing to write off the debt, but they are going to hang on to all of the bitterness? Does it mean that all of the hostility is still there, the suspiciousness and distrust? If you can relate to the lines of the poem, you'll see that there is a state of being, a quality of spirituality, from which true forgiveness comes that can set us free. The mind-set that allows forgiveness is a lot more than some intellectual decision that says, "I am going to forget this nightmare so I can move on." The spiritual framework has to be there or it doesn't work.

The poem ends with some beautiful advice for all of us recovering adult children. When we are sick and tired of being dead, when we have had enough of carrying around the price of resentment, we want to be free. We want to be washed up from our grave so that we can see beauty and experience love. No matter how great the abuse that was done to us in the past, we simply refuse to carry it with us through each day of our lives. So after having this breakthrough, this spiritual experience, we become ready to embrace some new truths. This is the advice the poem "Renascence" offers.

> *The world stands out on either side*
> *No wider than the heart is wide;*
> *Above the world is stretched the sky,—*
> *No higher than the soul is high.*
> *The heart can push the sea and land*
> *Farther away on either hand;*
> *The soul can split the sky in two,*

And let the face of God shine through.
But east and west will pinch the heart
That cannot keep them pushed apart;
And he whose soul is flat—the sky
Will cave in on him by and by.

Think about the image "he whose soul is flat." Isn't it true that when our souls and spirits are filled with resentment, anger, and hostility, we are missing out on life? Isn't it true that east and west will only be as far apart as our hearts *hold* them apart? Won't the sky only be as high as our souls will *let* it be high? The spirituality of forgiveness depends on an awareness of beauty as well as ugliness, of joy as well as pain. A negative, cranky, hostile, victim mentality about ourselves and about the world makes it almost impossible for us to forgive others.

How much of the negative, cranky, hostile, victim mentality are *you* carrying around? If, in fact, you are just as full of that as so many wounded people are, even if you intellectually make the decision to forgive, you will still have to *learn how* to forgive. There is some fundamental, roll-up-the-sleeves spiritual work that needs to be done. It is a primary task that can't simply be wrapped up in five or six steps, or outward behaviors. Readiness is a meditative, "inside" job. It is a state of spirituality, a spiritual plateau that we reach by thought and prayer and willingness. It's finally getting a look at the "big picture," and it is that totality that makes the difference. Why? Because the more we are riveted on the part, the less we are able to live in the whole. And the more we see that whole as negative, as hostile, as dangerous, the less able we are to see that the whole—our lives in the world—can by and large be benevolent. If we approach life as a friend, wonderful, friendly things come back to us. Are *you* friendlier than the world is to you? That's the primary question.

Now let's pick up with the idea we left off. Remember that the first item on the agenda of forgiveness is not about forgiving someone else—it's about putting our own minds in such a position that we *can* forgive. Our goal is to live in spiritual health. So what makes that so difficult? What keeps us from deciding to forgive and then just doing it? One reason is that it takes toughness. This task of developing a spiritual framework that will house forgiveness is heroic work. Challenging lifetime thinking habits is the task of heroes. It is not easy, simple stuff.

Mind-Sets That Block Forgiveness

What are some of the mind-sets that make forgiveness impossible, or at least extremely difficult? The first one is the mind-set that says **we don't deserve happiness**. We don't deserve to have our needs filled. We already know that we cannot have healthy boundaries around what we do not feel entitled to. So if we do not feel entitled to justice, happiness, or having our rights acknowledged, then, of course, we are going to have a terrible time forgiving. So we must accomplish that fundamental, primary work if we are going to effectively forgive.

Now, think about the second mind-set that says **we are owed**. Won't that always lock us in the throes of resentment? A lot of us have an exaggerated sense of what we think we are owed. For all of the identification and relief that recovery programs, literature, and meetings have facilitated, many people have found these parts of recovery dangerous and negative. And they *can* be. We can talk so much about what we were denied and deprived of that the implied, underlying premise seems to be that somehow we were owed perfect acceptance, perfect parents, and unconditional love. It's very easy for our just complaints to become exaggerated. People aren't perfect. Nobody gets unconditional love.

What we imagine we should have had may not even be real. The love we get is all a matter of degree. Hopefully, it's not so conditional that it cannot be had, but it's not perfect for anyone.

What do you perceive that you are owed? Can even the best people owe you something they do not have to give? In some mystical, cosmic sense, you may say, "Sure, whether they had it to give or not, I was owed it, and I got cheated." That may be true in some cosmic hall of justice, but in the real world, in a practical sense, can you reasonably hold other people accountable for not giving you what they did not have to give? There are many of us who come to the table of recovery, which inevitably is the table of forgiveness, accompanied by a handicapping mind-set about what was owed us and not delivered.

This seems to be an especially seductive mind-set for many of the younger generation. Somehow we adults have allowed and fostered a crippling mentality that sets up young people to feel they are owed *everything*. They're owed the unlimited resources of their parents; they're owed cars to drive around in; they're owed college educations; they're owed almost everything. How unfair to raise young people with the sense that somehow they are owed so much! It robs them of the independence and integrity of knowing that they can go out and make it on their own, that they are not going to have to lean on other people. It's unrealistic and unfair to lead children to such erroneous conclusions about what it takes to build a good life.

How realistic are your expectations of what *you* are owed? Many of us go to a group once or twice and never go back because we think the group was not friendly enough. Often our mind-set is, "If I come to a group, if I make all of this extraordinary effort to come, then by God, they owe it to me to enthusiastically reach out and make me feel welcome and wanted." And of course it *is* the group's responsibility to reach out—but the group doesn't *owe* us. We're going to that group because *we* hurt and because *we* are in need. The more unrealistic our sense of being owed is, the more we're going to feel cheated, the more resentment we're going to have, and the more hurt we're going to feel.

The third mind-set that gets in the way of forgiveness is that fantasy idea of **instant gratification**. "If I am going to pray to God at eight o'clock," we say, "by eight-fifteen I had better have this spiritual experience that I hear about and some great relief right along with it." Well, that's a dangerous mind-set, because progress doesn't come quickly. We may not get any relief immediately. It can take time. That's why spiritual progress can't be had without mental toughness. We've got to be tough to hang in there for whatever time it takes to make it happen. And we've got to be willing to fill up that time with plenty of repeated, effective behavior. Instant gratification is a pipe dream.

The mind-set that works instead is, "I'm here for the long haul." Relative to forgiveness, which is recovery, our attitude can be, "I'm here for as long as it takes. I'm going to stick at it and keep going until it does happen." All the success stories that people tell, the tales of wonderful relief from resentment and a new ability to forgive, sometimes don't make clear that it has taken them five to ten years or even longer to get there. Perhaps we don't hear them saying that it took every single day of praying and practicing new ways to become as alive as they are today. But it did. Instant gratification is not a mind-set that is going to make spiritual forgiveness happen. There is a big difference between rational forgiveness and spiritual forgiveness. The people who have "arrived" got there because they were tough enough to stay with it.

Here is a fourth mind-set that can be an absolute killer: **we are run by our feelings**. If we are run by our feelings, we will probably never forgive. If we have really been cheated and damaged, our feelings of hostility and resentment can so dominate us that we can't get in touch with any other part of ourselves—like the intellectual part, the behavior part, the "acting as if" part. If we are too driven by our feelings, then anger and resentment and hostility will exclusively call the shots. *They* are in control; *we* are not.

A man in a meeting said, "Who's the boss here?" And he was talking to himself! He felt very frightened about doing a particular behavior that flew in the face of his codependent mind-set. He had been offered a promotion and a pay raise. But his mind-set told him, "You are never going to succeed. You don't deserve to succeed. You are never going to be better than what you are." He had enormous fear, and yet he really wanted this promotion. He deserved the promotion. He knew he could perform well in the new job. "I just sat there," he said, "and I went within. I said, 'Hey, who's the boss here? Is it me or is it this old fear?' " Recognizing that it was nothing more than his old fear coming back on him from the past, he said he rejected it. It was a wonderful story that lit up the whole meeting. He was tough enough to overcome the obstacle and, therefore, he got the reward. Facing down our fear is no easy thing. Fear, like anger, has a very loud voice. Only toughness gets the job done.

The fifth mind-set that presents an enormous obstacle to spiritual forgiveness is that **we expect that it will be easy**. Somehow we imagine that this whole process of regaining wholeness and health is nothing more than solving an intellectual puzzle or untangling a few emotional knots. How well we know that in every area of human endeavor, success takes concerted, consistent effort over months and years. Whether it's learning to play the piano or running a marathon or performing brain surgery, we accept that we've got to stick with the learning and pay the price. It's not easy, but we have to do it. Yet somehow, when it comes to personal growth and recovery issues, we tell ourselves that if it doesn't happen easily and quickly, then we aren't going to do it. Genuine personal growth is never easy. The kind of toughness it takes, especially if there has been some major-league abuse in our lives, is terribly demanding. But the reward is no less than our bedrock quality of life. And we can pass these lessons on to our children and to all of the people around us. We can't give what we don't have. The mentality of the quick fix gets in the way of forgiveness.

What *is* easy is saying, "You don't understand. My case is exceptional." If we have recently learned that our husband or wife has been having a long-term affair, or if we were literally tortured as a child, we may well feel entitled to excuse ourselves from the rules and guidelines that apply to people who weren't hurt so badly. There are many situations that, for all the rational reasons in the world, we can use to justify refusing forgiveness. We can make a good case for sitting on the resentment and not even thinking about moving toward the spiritual level of forgiveness. And of course it's up to us whether or not we are even going to attempt to move toward it. Only *we* can decide whether the effort is worth it. But at least we should understand that if we stay focused around that hurt, as justifiable as that may feel, then we are stuck. To move on takes mental toughness. And it takes time.

Check yourself out against the obstacles to mental and spiritual forgiveness: the codependency that says you don't deserve to be happy; the mind-sets of feeling owed, of instant gratification, of being run by your feelings, of expecting that forgiveness should be easy. How many of these obstacles are causing you problems in achieving forgiveness?

Why Forgive?

It helps to not only take a look at what forgiveness is, but also what it is not. Remember that forgiving ourselves is first a matter of dealing with our underlying mind-set and developing an overall forgiving attitude. But we also need to address the issue of forgiving others. In both cases, forgiveness has nothing to do with *them*. It simply doesn't make sense for us to say, "I am not even going to try to forgive until they are worth it. I will work at forgiving when they say they are sorry. I will work at forgiveness when somehow they communicate to me that they realize and regret what they have done."

Doesn't that give *them* all of *our* power? What if they never apologize? What if they are never sorry? What if they are never even capable of knowing what they did to us? Then what? Then what do we do? We are still letting them dictate the quality of our lives. And the whole point of this work is to acknowledge how tragic it was that this abuse ever happened at all, but even worse to let it happen every day of our lives when, today, it is our choice not to let it happen. We didn't have any power or control over what happened to us when we were four, five, six, seven, or eight years old. But we do have a choice now whether we are going to keep on carrying that hurt and resentment with us. It is up to us. We simply can't afford to base our efforts at forgiveness on what we are willing to expend on the people who hurt us. The key to forgiveness is the realization that the price we are paying for the resentment is simply too high. The goal is to refuse to pay this price any longer. That is why we forgive. It's for ourselves; it is not about them. It is about our own quality of life.

We can't afford to base our forgiveness decisions on anyone but ourselves. Some people are not in recovery; some people are not capable of understanding abuse. Some people are not able to say, "I'm sorry," even if they really are sorry. They are simply not capable of reaching out to you even if you reach out to them first; they don't know how. None of those conditions has any real bearing on whether you are going to forgive or not.

The Eight Steps to Forgiveness

So what do we do once we've decided to move on to a spiritual level of forgiveness? How do we do it?

The first step is **choosing our intention**. "Intention" means that we make up our minds, whether we feel like it or not, to make a good, clear mental decision that we want to forgive. The truth is that a lot of us flatly don't want to forgive. We want to go right on plotting exquisite revenge on that dirty rotten dog that did us wrong. Are *you* at a point where even intellectually you're able to say, "Yes, I want to forgive. I may not feel it, but I want to." Not because *they* are or are not deserving of it, but because *you* are deserving of it. We forgive because it damages us if we don't. That's the first step, the intention step. Do you have the intention—have you made the decision—that you want to move beyond resentment and hostility?

The **paying attention** step comes next. Paying attention means staying on it, keeping at it. We can benefit greatly by paying attention to daily disciplines; being mindful of what our thoughts are, what our behavior is, where our feelings are leading us. Are you paying attention? As you think about where your attention is, it may be enlightening to think about this: before you really started to focus on the facts about anger, forgiveness, and reconciliation, how constant and frequent were your thoughts of resentment and revenge? Notice the close attention you were paying to the damage that was done to you and the resultant hurt, sadness, and grief. Many, many people pay attention to their grievances every minute of every hour of every day for years. That's why their sense of grievance is so strong. When we've paid that much attention to our pain, doesn't it simply make sense that we'll have to pay just as much attention to moving off in another direction? The whole process of forgiveness and reconciliation is step by step. It requires keeping our minds on the job. Unlike the poem where the woman said a prayer and the clouds dumped down rain and washed her out of the ground, major changes don't happen all at once. We have to pay attention to do the work.

The third step is **taking consistent action**. Like what? Since forgiveness and reconciliation begin in our own heads, in our own lives, we must start with ourselves. So whether we ever approach someone else or not, we need to first of all *think it*. If you cannot say these thoughts out loud, run them through your head: "I am free of resentment. I choose to live a life of spiritual growth. I don't have to live with all of this resentment and hurt and negativity. It is my choice." Admit to yourself that life is not fair. Tell yourself what you know is true: "I was cheated. I was abused. I didn't get what I needed. Life is not fair, but today's choice is mine."

Perhaps you can form statements in your mind, even if you don't say them out loud, like: "For my sake, Dad or Mother or whoever, for my sake, I forgive you." Nobody has to know that you are doing this. You may be waiting for a bus, but you can be working on it mentally. Suppose you have carried around resentment for many years toward your parents because they did not give you what you needed. Now, in your mental workout, you can think past the hurt and pain and focus on how little they may have had to give. Mentally, this begins to plow the ground. First of all, you are daring to even think the thought, "I want to forgive." If you can't think about your parents' faces yet, envision your own face free of the anger, free of the resentment, free of the hostility. See that in your mind. See what that looks like.

Number four is **saying it out loud**. At first, the best place to try this is in the privacy of your own home, perhaps in your own bathroom with the door locked. But begin to say and hear yourself say, "I forgive." Tell yourself, "I choose freedom." Look right in that mirror and say, "I deserve to be free." Remember that forgiveness has to first be seeded in the plowed ground of your own spirit. So if you get terribly down on yourself about something that you think you should have done better, look in the mirror and tell yourself, "I did the best I could." After thinking it in the previous step, maybe now you will be able to verbalize out loud, "My parents did the best they could. They gave me all they had."

Some of you who have been sexually abused or physically battered will have trouble simply telling yourself that your parents did the best they could. That position is not believable if there has been terrible abuse and hurt and damage. In those situations, perhaps you can tell yourself that you deserve to forgive for your own sake. The important thing is to practice verbalizing it out loud. Whatever we do often enough, whatever we think about often enough, becomes normal. It becomes who we are.

Once you become comfortable with the thought and then with the private verbalization, you are ready to practice saying it to someone else. At your meetings or with a trusted friend, begin to verbalize to another human being. Perhaps you could say something like, "I really do want to forgive, but at the same time I want vengeance so bad that I can hardly sleep at night and my stomach is in a knot. But in spite of all that, I sincerely want to forgive." Up until now it may be that all of your verbalizing to other people has been limited to justifying the gripe. And the more you justified it and the more you verbalized it, the more you owned it. But you can now start to verbalize about forgiveness and reconciliation. Start to verbalize about moving on beyond the anger and the hurt. That's where the power is. So begin to say it to other people as well as yourself.

Number five is a tough one, but perhaps it is time to begin **saying something to the per-**

son that you have the resentment or the hurt toward. Maybe first you can speak out in a letter. Maybe you'd be more comfortable on the phone. There are many different ways to make the first approach. The important thing is, *just do it.* So many of us have said that when we finally talked straight to the other person, when at last we shared our true feelings, the sense of relief and the sense of freedom we experienced since have been astounding. Of course, this freedom wasn't going to happen until the pieces were put into place. Before we can say to someone else, "No, this is not all right," or "That really hurt me," or "I'm not okay with this," we first have to say it to ourselves. And usually we cannot say it to ourselves until we are first willing to think it.

Some people pooh-pooh baby steps. Just sitting quietly at home or on the bus and beginning to think certain thoughts is a pretty small beginning step, all right. But it may be the only step that is possible to begin with—especially if we're all choked off with anger and hurt and resentment. Any step and every step count. Thinking it, verbalizing it to ourselves, and then verbalizing it to somebody else leads to actually confronting that person. Once we sit down face-to-face in some kind of neutral environment, perhaps we can begin to verbalize clearly and forcefully with that other person, and we can even begin to set some healthy boundaries.

The psychology of habit is that whatever we do often enough is going to become the norm; it's going to become who we are. Maybe it's time we sit down and begin to write in a journal. One fellow said he got free of anger by taking the time to make two lists. One list gave all the reasons he was angry at his brother, and the other showed the part that he, the list-maker, had played in these injustices. Those lists, he said, shed new light. Before, he had totally blamed his brother for a lot of the misery of his youth. Making the lists led him to understand that it wasn't *all* his brother's fault. Writing it down enabled the man to take ownership of his part of the problem, to intellectually forgive, and to spiritually let go. When he began to act on this, he began to make progress.

Here is the sixth action step: **Smiling at people.** Remember that negative, cranky, hostile, victim-mentality people are carrying around resentments that prevent an attitude of forgiveness. One way to start turning that around is to come up with a kind word for other people. As homely as this advice sounds, it gets magical results; we can begin to give people smiles rather than frowns. We can consistently ask a question about what is going on in someone else's life and then be quiet and listen. Many of us habitually talk only about ourselves, or we're so withdrawn we never really talk to anybody about anything. And then we wonder why we're so lonely, so full of anger, so plagued by hostility and resentments. Well, nobody wants to be around us! So maybe the consistent behavior we need to practice is the friendly approach.

Another way to be kind is by giving people the benefit of the doubt. It's not easy to do on a daily, consistent basis. Suppose we are thinking about some gloomy situation, either nationally or personally, something sad or disastrous that happened. The last thing we may feel like doing is giving some stranger the benefit of the doubt. It takes an act of will to tell ourselves that every kid with long hair is probably not on drugs or selling drugs, or that every person who runs into us did not do it on purpose. When we are driving home and we see that long-haired young person out there wearing weird clothes, we can remind ourselves that appearances can be deceiving. How do we know who he is, what he values? The point is to challenge and act against our negative, knee-jerk patterns. As we act, we shall be.

What are the kind actions that *you* need to take? A man named Wes, because his family taught him that life was dangerous and everyone was out to get him, expressed his hostility behind the wheel. He would *never* let anyone cut in front of him. And if someone did somehow manage to cut in front of him, he simply saw red. Chances are he would tailgate that car and honk his horn and try to cut in front of it the first chance he got. Since he's been working on forgiveness, Wes said he's been reevaluating his driving habits. Every time he goes out on the road now he said he forces himself to let at least two people cut in front of him. Allowing that is simply an exercise of torment for him. Yet he realizes now that other drivers are not out to get him even if they behave in an impolite, discourteous way. "Why would I give them the power to make me so nervous and upset? Let them be who they want to be, and I will be who I want to be. I choose not to be a jerk." We can make giant gains from such small, everyday decisions, if we back up those decisions with action.

The seventh action step is a critical one: **Praying.** We need to make conscious contact with God, as we understand God to be. In the area of forgiveness, there is no substitute for prayerful preparation. The odds of overcoming long-term resentments, especially if they are great, are not in our favor. The battle is too fierce if ours is the only power we have ᵗo win it. Our own power is not enough.

Prayer fits in the consistent action category. Do *you* make contact with God, as you understand God to be, on a daily basis? In humble supplication, do you ask for the power to be free of the hurt and the resentment and the grief and the rage at the injustice in your life? How often do you do that? In contrast, how often during the day do you have thoughts that fortify and cement your resentments? Do you have angry feelings on a daily basis? Then why wouldn't it take a daily effort to reverse that whole mental framework?

Some of us say, "I take three minutes in the morning and, boy, in that short little time I do my daily reading and prayer!" Of course, *any* number of minutes a day is wonderful, but how many minutes during the day do we spend in self-pity? How many minutes of the day do we plan revenge? How many times during the day do we think hostile, negative, suspicious thoughts? Stack up all of that time next to the three minutes and which way do you think the battle will go?

The prayer we need is more like a constant state of mind than it is a quick recital of words. This doesn't mean that we seek saintly perfection or that we get so paranoid about praying "correctly" that we drive ourselves mad. It means that we must become aware that help is *always* there so we can put ourselves in the presence of God many times during the day. Perhaps we say the Third or Eleventh Step of AA, or we visualize an image that means something to us. One woman recently told her group about a beautiful statue she had of a little child resting in the protection of a cupped hand. To her, this statue symbolized the hand of God protecting her, comforting her, loving her.

What image or poem or Step or saying would help you maintain conscious contact? What would remind you that it isn't just you against the world; it's you and God. Together, there is nothing that the two of you can't overcome. Conscious contact with the God of your understanding is crucial because the goal of forgiveness and letting go are spiritual realities.

The eighth and last of the concrete action steps is **talking straight**. Low self-esteem always has to do with sacrificing our integrity, and many times this loss of integrity comes from our not talking straight. Anytime we don't talk straight or we aren't honest for the sake of being accepted or for the sake of being liked or for the sake of trying to recapture some of the acceptance and love that we didn't get as a child, we are giving away a little piece of our integrity. When we don't ask for what we need or tell people how we feel, we are setting snares in our own path.

And sooner or later, every one of those snares will trip us up. In a very real sense, healthy self-esteem is the seedbed of truly healing forgiveness.

How consistently do you talk straight? How skilled are you at speaking your truth? How often have you set snares in your own path? When you are talking with people, whether it is business or a personal conversation, are you clear? Do you mince words or just say right out how you feel and what you want? Suppose you're talking to your spouse or partner. Do you really want to build another big addition on your house even though it is going to leave you financially strapped? What do you really want? Do you really want to go to the ballet or do you really want to go to the wrestling match? What is it that you want to do? Do you talk straight? This doesn't mean that you should demand that you always get your way. Your self-esteem is not based on always getting your own way, but it *is* based on talking straight. That's the way integrity expresses itself.

Suppose someone lays out a plan and asks you if it's okay. If the plan is not really okay with you, do you say it? We have many reasons for holding back on our own opinions, like wanting to be accepted and wanting to be approved of. If we're dependent on other people's opinions, we'll say anything is all right when it is really not all right.

How do you answer if somebody asks, "Is this fair?" How easy is it for you to say that something is *not* fair? Most of us want to be the agreeable, lovable good guy. Most people hate conflict. But if you are sacrificing your integrity to be accepted, you're jeopardizing your self-esteem and will have a very hard time with forgiveness and reconciliation. What do you say when somebody asks how you really feel? Do you automatically say, "Fine," whether you feel fine or not? What is the truth? Have you spent days or months or even years with a knot in your stomach because you so badly wanted to say something that you couldn't quite get out? Were you burning to say, "I don't approve of this," or "I don't want to be in this business anymore," or "I really care about you." If there is an opinion or an emotion or a truth you need to express, *not* saying it is costing you a lot. If you habitually withhold your opinions and feelings, your self-esteem is going to be on the floor. And that makes it terribly difficult to affect true spiritual forgiveness. Every day that you don't talk straight, the situation gets worse.

If you take these eight steps, you begin to put your muscles where your mouth is. By such small moves forward, you can begin to develop an *attitude* of forgiveness from which an *act* of true healing and spiritual forgiveness can come. Then comes reconciliation.

5 ✧ ✧ ✧

Reconciliation
with Family

In a real sense, this chapter on reconciliation is the payoff of this whole book. What could we want more than to rebuild the bridges that were burned in our past? Clearly there is enormous satisfaction in being able to go back, reach out, and reestablish those connections that wasted so much of our love and infected us with so much anger.

How our ears perk up when people at meetings tell about their attempts at reconciliation—sometimes with their family as a whole, sometimes with a specific parent, sometimes with siblings, sometimes with grandparents. Some of these stories are beautiful and thrilling. You can just see the people straining to adequately express how absolutely wonderful it was to set up this reconciliation, to sit face-to-face and talk to whomever it was who hurt them. They tell of forgiveness and tears and sometimes surprise because the people on the other side of the table didn't even know the person was carrying resentment. They didn't know that the adult child was wounded by some attitude or situation.

One woman was amazed when her mother said, "If I would have known that this was hurting you, I would have done it differently. I'm sorry." One man's parent had always said, "You can do better," which the man interpreted as meaning that nothing he did was good enough, that he was being picked on, that he was always being taught shame. Then, in the confrontation, when the reconciliation finally happened, the parent said, "I always loved you. I was just trying to make you aware that you could do better, that you could be the best. You were such a wonderful little boy. I wanted to make sure that you didn't settle for second best." Sometimes just uncovering the intention of the parent who hurt you is enough to effect wonderful reconciliation.

But other reconciliation stories contain some of the most painful sentiments imaginable because the attempted reconciliation didn't work. Sometimes it didn't work because not only was there no forgiveness, but there was more punishment and more rejection. In other cases, it didn't work because the person attempting the reconciliation either had outlandish expectations or something else went awry. Successful reconciliation is largely a matter of readiness. First, we have to get ready by forgiving ourselves, life, and the other person. So how then do we begin to build bridges? How can we most effectively try to reestablish the connections that either were broken or that never existed? How does that happen? What makes the difference between reconciliation attempts that work and those that don't? What are the principles? That's what this chapter is all about.

The Principles of Reconciliation

Reconciliation first of all requires that we have things squared away within ourselves. The quality of our reaching out is always dependent on the quality of the center that we reach out *from*. The more we are able to integrate within our personality all the positives and negatives of our lives, what is healthy and what is unhealthy within us become a solid whole. The integrity of our inner self very much dictates the quality of how we reach out.

Perhaps this means moving from being passive-aggressive to simply being aggressive, if that's what the situation calls for. This means that we have climbed out of that game of not asking for what we need until our frustration explodes sideways on people who have less power. It means that there has been some healing of all that passive-aggressive nonsense, and we have made some real movement toward being assertive. It means that people can count on us, that we are becoming more even tempered, that people don't have to wonder when they talk to us whether they are going to get Dr. Jekyll or Mr. Hyde.

Self-reconciliation means we have moved from satisfying our needs at the expense of others to satisfying our needs legitimately. A typical unreconciled adult child will try to satisfy his or her needs—because they are so deep and because there has been so much hurt—at the expense of other people. Often, we lead people on, seducing them toward us, and then when they no longer fit, we reject them; we push them away. It's the classic seduction-rejection process. Integration and self-reconciliation mean that we have grown out of people-pleasing and moved on to self-pleasing. Isn't that a wonderful concept? How many times in our lives have we eroded our integrity by people-pleasing? How often were we willing to do almost anything to get acceptance? Didn't our whole lives revolve around not getting other people angry at us? Didn't we become slaves to whatever it took to belong, to finally being part of the "in crowd"? And, of course, the more we prostituted ourselves for acceptance, the less we were accepted. In comparison to the price we paid, there was never any real acceptance, never any real friendship, never any real feeling that we were at home.

Self-pleasing means that we know what we want to do. What activities are fun for us and how often do we do them? Do we have a sense of boundaries around what reasonable bending and compromising we should do to be part of a group? Do we know where to draw the line so we can say, "If I have to cross this line to be accepted by you, then you aren't worth it or your acceptance isn't worth it"? That's what it takes to establish those healthy boundaries, which is what reconciliation within ourselves is all about.

Or how about this one? Have we moved from needing to control other people and outcomes toward a healthier stance of live and let live? Suppose people are doing something that we don't like. Is their behavior a big enough deal that we need to go to war? Must we control the quality and the modality of other people's lives to the extent that we reject them if they don't fall under our power? Do they either have to do it our way or have nothing to do with us? If our need to be in control is still strong, when we come to the reconciliation table to reach out to someone else, we are likely to say that we will reconcile *only* as long as it is on our own terms. And, chances are, it isn't going to be on our terms. It isn't going to be exactly as we wanted or as we fantasized it was going to be.

How about this one? Reconciliation within ourselves means that we have moved from codependency in sexual relationships to a healthier kind of love. If you are a man, perhaps that means that you have moved from the kind of codependency that does not allow a woman to have her own thoughts or her own opinions, that makes you unable to tolerate a woman as an equal. Or perhaps your codependency is such that if you are not at all times in a relationship with a woman in a significant sexual way, you somehow feel that you are less of a man, that your life is worthless. Have you gotten rid of all those knee-jerk, codependent "truisms" that you learned somewhere along the way? If there has been reconciliation within yourself, you have overcome enough codependency to allow you to have a genuine friendship with a woman. You can function as a true partner with your significant other without requiring that person to be your servant or your maid. Reconciliation with self means you have healthy boundaries around your relationship with women.

Another test of reconciliation within ourselves is to ask this: have we moved from pity to love? How often adult children confuse pity with love! Oftentimes, our whole role in life is to make somebody else's life wonderful. We must be sorry for every negative thing that happens to that person without thinking about all the negative, painful things that are happening to *us*. So many times we adult children buy into that role because that's what we were taught and what we grew up with. By having unbalanced, unbounded pity on the other person, we formed terrible boundaries around where other people's responsibility starts and ours ends. Endless pity was all there was. We learned that the only way there was any chance of acceptance or love in any kind of a relationship was by absolutely bending over backward to make someone else's life better. That's why we confuse pity with love. Compassion is an absolutely wonderful virtue, but not when we get confused and translate pity into loyalty toward untrustworthy people. All that can happen in that scenario is that we get terribly hurt. When we reconcile with self, we know that we can have compassion for someone else without falling in love with that person and then being a victim of that love.

Have we moved from a bottomless pit of need to a stronger position that allows us to give and get legitimate love? The never-ending search for love in our lives creates an enormous deficit within us, which explains why so many of us adult children confuse our need to be held with our ability to love and be loved. That confusion results in dependent relationships. We become emotionally dependent on the other person to our tremendous detriment. If we have not reconciled with self, which means that we have not healed enough to distinguish between need and love, it's not hard to imagine what's going to happen when we try to reach out for any kind of effective reconciliation with others. It's going to be absolutely chaotic.

Take the case of a very stressed out man who came into his group saying, "I need your help; I need your help." Someone said, "Well, what's wrong?" And he blurted out, "My girlfriend left town on a business trip yesterday, so I called up this old girlfriend of mine, and we got together, and now she won't leave. She says if I won't have her for a significant friend, she is going to commit suicide! I don't want her to commit suicide, but I've got to get her out of there. What am I going to do?" What a fix he was in! One of the group members said, "Well, hold it, hold it. Wait a second. Let's go back to the beginning. Let me ask you something. This girlfriend who left town—are you in a committed relationship with her? You know, an exclusive, committed relationship?" In a very distracted kind of

144

way he said, "Yeah, sure, sure, sure." When the group asked why he had called up this old girlfriend in the first place, he simply said, "Well, I got lonely. I needed somebody's arms around me." His unreconciled need for acceptance and intimacy set him up for devastation. Suppose this man desperately wanted to reach out for reconciliation with other people. Would he have success? How deep and complete is his own personal integrity? It's faulty. It's flawed. It's weak. *How well we've done with ourselves determines how well we'll do with other people.* What's the difference between those attempts at reconciliation that work and those that don't? To a large extent, the difference is in the attitude of the person reaching out, the one who's trying to effect the reconciliation.

Another important prerequisite for reconciliation is to have moved from illegitimate or flawed "respect" for our parents to owning our own adulthood. Many of us adult children act out "respect" for our parents by mindlessly bending to them. This kind of submissive attitude can never effect a reconciliation. If we have grown up, then we owe adulthood to ourselves. Giving respect to our parents does not mean that we owe them our brains, our serenity, or our peace of mind. But telling the difference between true respect and flawed respect isn't always easy.

There was a man in a group who was almost sick to death because his tiny eighty-four-year-old father was coming to visit him. Because of illegitimate respect, he always had to sacrifice his integrity whenever he spent time with his father. He would have to do things that he didn't want to do. Where is the line between respect for our parents and ownership of our own adulthood? Finding that balance is the important thing; moving from perfectionism toward acceptance and satisfaction with doing our best. All we can do is our best.

We don't seek perfection; we seek progress. These are two completely different things. Have we reconciled that, or do we still have a need—for all the adult children reasons—to be perfect? Is nothing we do ever done well enough? Many of us who are hurt by attempted reconciliations that didn't work are coming from the standpoint of perfectionism. If the reconnection doesn't come out perfectly—which means exactly as we think it should—we think it didn't work. But this isn't what reconciliation is all about; it's about *knowing we did all we could*. It's as much about the attempt as it is about the result. If we have made the best attempt that we could after thoroughly preparing ourselves, even if the others were not able to respond in any kind of a healthy way—we won.

We did the mature, healing, spiritual thing. So it was successful as far as we were concerned. How good we feel about it all depends on the inner state of reconciliation within ourselves.

Moving from deliberate lose-lose situations to realistic risk taking has a great impact on our attempted reconciliation. Many of us adult children have learned that whatever we try to do is not going to work, that we are always going to fail, that nothing is ever good enough. This gives us a lot of experience in confusing absolutely hopeless, lose-lose situations with legitimate risk taking. But what good is an attempt at reconciliation that is guaranteed to lose, guaranteed to cause even more pain at the end than what we had at the start? That's not legitimate risk taking. That's just buying into the same old adult child lose-lose mentality and renaming it "recovery" or "reconciliation." And it's not.

What is our *expectation* if we are about to reach out to others who may not be able to reach back to us? If we expect that the success of this effort is going to depend on the other people fully understanding and hearing what we say, we may be very disappointed. If we count on them to respond at all to whatever it is we need to say, then we are dreaming. It is very unlikely to happen. That's not what reconciliation is about. To demand that others give us what they may well not have to give is not "recovery," not "help," not "holy." It's just the same old adult child stuff acted out under the name of recovery. We owe ourselves and others realistic expectations. How much can they give back to us? Have we grown out of that defeating adult child lose-lose behavior that sabotages our success? Have we become able to do some legitimate, honest risk taking? Do we know the difference?

Reconciliation within ourselves requires that we know the difference between "dwell on" and "deal with." Do we endlessly dwell on a hurt? To incessantly dwell on a situation that caused us pain is not the same as dealing with it. To tell ourselves over and over and over that if we can't get reconciliation, our lives are only half-lives is not the same thing as dealing with the issues that broke the bridges in the first place. Dealing with our lives means putting those issues behind us—which of course can mean a lot of things. If reconciliation is effective, and we are able to have a healthier, more loving relationship with our parents and our families, then fine. That allows us to put the hurt behind us, enjoy what we have regained, and get on with our lives. But if, after all our best attempts at reconciliation, it is clear that *there is not going to be* a healthy, loving relationship with our parents or our families because they flatly aren't up to it—they don't have it—then all we can do is let it go. In that case, "put it behind us" means that we stop trying to get blood from a rock. We stop basing the success and the health of our own lives on the quality of our families because it is not there to be had, it is not going to happen. In both cases, the difference between "dwelling on" and "dealing with" our own issues determines the reconciliation that has been accomplished within ourselves. That's the source from which every successful effort is going to come.

Once we have honestly dealt with reconciliation within ourselves, however, it's time to reach back past the broken bridge and try to salvage whatever we can. So what are the steps in doing that? How does that happen? For starters, it's important to understand that any attempt at reconciliation with others *requires some kind of confrontation*. The hurt, the loss, the abuse that happened to us have to be addressed head-on. It's a necessity that we become willing to kick a very dangerous kind of sleeping dog. Before we do it, we have to make sure it's worth it.

We have to be certain that we're willing to accept the results of this confrontation. We have to be willing to relive some of that pain—because if it doesn't come to the surface, there isn't going to be any reconciliation. Reconciliation is not about people-pleasing. Reconciliation is not about submerging our thoughts and our feelings and somehow reaching out desperately to make a connection with these other people. That isn't going to work. That hell-bent, headlong approach will only create more anger and more hurt and more pain. Reconciliation is a much deeper reality that's about confronting what was inappropriate in the past. It requires straight talk about how we feel and about what was taken away from us or lost. The rewards may be great, but it is devilishly hard work.

Reconciliation requires a great deal of honesty. If we are going to make a genuine attempt, then "halfway" doesn't count. Veiled hints are not going to make it work. If there is going to be a legitimate try at reconciliation, the approach has to be head-on and up-front. The other people have to know what we are talking about, and *we* must know what we want to say. The only good reason to confront what was wrong in the past is because this is very, very important to us.

The Steps Toward Reconciliation

Suppose we are willing to do whatever it takes. Then what are the specific, concrete steps that we must take? The first step toward reconciliation might well be stated, **Go with your head, not just with your heart—** regardless of how much you want "home," regardless of how badly you want reconciliation. Reconciliation cannot be healthier or more complete than the people involved. So first ask yourself if your family has changed. Are they in recovery? Are they open to the kind of reconciliation that you are talking about? Do they even want it? Go with your head when you're giving yourself answers. Some of us with good intentions are terribly hurt because we wanted to reconcile so badly that we blindly walked back into situations that had not changed one iota from where we started twenty or thirty years ago. As abusive and as hurtful as it was then, the situation was still exactly the same. We were the only ones who changed. Nothing and no one else was one bit different. Are the people you want to reconcile with different? Have they changed? Do you have any real hope that reconciliation is possible?

There's no way to overestimate the importance of expectations. If you know deep in your heart that there is no logical hope of reconciliation, then maybe your whole agenda is not about reconciliation, but about *your speaking the truth to them*, whether they can hear or accept it or not. Wishful thinking about getting some marvelous response from people who are not in recovery, who have not changed, who, chances are, have just gotten older and more set in their ways, only sets you up to be devastated. So the point is not to give up on it or call it off, but to go in there with your eyes open. Go in there as realistically as you possibly can.

The second step is to understand that **family systems, like all systems, seek stability.** And there are some family systems that will only tolerate sickness. If you have a family system that will only tolerate sickness, you must understand that the whole energy of that system goes to maintaining the status quo. The unspoken mandate is to *keep things as they are.* So what can you reasonably expect if you confront an unrecovered family system? You can expect that that family system is going to tighten up to protect the regular, ordinary flow of that system. All of the early codependency is going to spring into action and show its face in full bloom. The people-pleasers in that system are going to act out to try to protect the feelings of everybody except you. The caretakers are going to act out by taking responsibility for saving everyone but you from feeling pain.

Suppose you've privately talked to a family member sometime before this reconciliation attempt, let's say your sister. Perhaps she told you about her own pain, or agreed with you that some event of the past was sick and abusive. Don't be surprised if, when she is around other family members in this system, she denies ever saying it. Or even if she doesn't deny it, she may say that you really didn't understand what she meant, when you know very well what she meant. It was as clear as the nose on your face. The great likelihood is that if she hasn't been working on her own personal recovery, if she hasn't done the work that you have done, then she is going to come forth in whatever way fits, especially when the family system is around.

Suppose the whole family system has activated around "protecting Dad." The consensus approach of that whole family system is, "Let's not tell Dad because he may get hurt, or he may get mad, or he's the one who has all the power and if we make him angry, he will withdraw his approval." If all that kind of old stuff has been in place for years, and if there has not been recovery, of course the same thing is going to happen during the reconciliation. It's a sure thing. So *expect* that it is going to happen because to not expect it is to set yourself up for failure. So take a heavy look. Are the people you are talking about, the family system, already changing and ready to change some more? Are they in recovery? Remember that *the family system is going to seek stability.* If the people are not in recovery, you must have realistic expectations about what is likely and unlikely to happen.

The third step is to sit down and **make a serious, honest list of everyone that you would like to reconcile with.** Is it an individual? Is it your whole family? Who is it? After each one of those names, write a paragraph about that person in terms of what changes may or may not have taken place in his or her life. Would the person *want* to reconcile with you? Is he or she open to the kind of reconciliation you have in mind? What might be and probably will be the person's reaction to you about this? This simple exercise takes your reconciliation plan out of the realm of "wouldn't it be nice?" It takes it out of the realm of hopes and dreams and wishes, and gives it some real flesh-and-blood reality.

One woman doing this exercise had wonderful visions of reestablishing and building a supportive, satisfying relationship with her mother. But as she wrote her paragraph out, she realized that her mother was eighty years old, beginning to suffer from Alzheimer's disease, had never gotten into recovery, and was codependent and dysfunctional for the past forty to fifty years of her life. In fantasy, the daughter thought she could go back and confront this sick old lady with her terrible parenting, with the fact that she did not protect her daughter from an alcoholic father. The truth was that the woman couldn't even protect herself from her alcoholic husband, let alone protect anybody else. She had no support group, she didn't have the foggiest understanding of what her options were. And now the mother was sick and eighty years old; she hardly knew what day of the week it was. But until the daughter did this exercise, she imagined she was going to go back and effect this wonderful, harmonious, tearful reunion. It was absolutely not possible.

Another person doing this exercise said his father was not alcoholic but was "very cruel." The father was dogmatic, dictatorial, had a short fuse, was horrendously full of rage and anger, and had been all of his life. The son said he could write a book on the varieties of abuse that he suffered as a child. For years and years the son suffered crushing nonacceptance and hurt feelings at the hands of his father. Well, the old man hadn't changed. He had only gotten older and angrier, more isolated and more frightened. The son said he still chose to reconcile, but not to confront his father, because he knew his father didn't have much to give. He knew that his father had treated him better than his father had been treated as a kid. As bad as it was, his father gave the best he had. So the son decided not to go back and confront this man about his miserable parenting, but to simply say, "Dad, I really do care about you. I really do love you. I don't know how much time we have left, but I would like us to be closer; I would like us to be better friends."

Somehow that approach touched a chord in the old man, who had never once shared any feelings with his son. Thus the son had no real evidence of how lonely and hurt his father was; he only guessed that this must be the case. So he felt there was no point in saying, "You hurt me terribly, and you had no right to do that." When the son did this exercise, he got a much clearer picture of who his father was. As a result, *he chose to go for what he thought he could get*, and there was quite a wonderful reconciliation effected. The old man was able to reach out to his son for the first time, and even to halfway apologize by saying, "I suppose I should have talked to you more." That was as good as he could do. While it wasn't exactly an apology, it was an acknowledgement that maybe things could have been better.

Many people who share their stories about

their reconciliation attempts clearly reflect that the success or failure of their efforts has to do not only with the state of reconciliation within themselves, but with their understanding of who the other person is. Oftentimes, even if the result is not the wished-for ideal, *things are much better than they were*. Some kind of bridge is at least established. To some degree, the wasted love is salvaged. How much do you know about the people you are trying to reconcile with? If you are going to reach back to them, what is the strongest and most hopeful way to do that? What is the most honest way? What can they hear and what can they not hear? What is your motivation? Is your goal revenge and punishment, or is it to establish some kind of honest relationship? Remember, there is always room for tact. Just beating people up in the name of honesty is not good. Think of the least abusive way to speak your truth. Don't people-please, don't deny your truth, but simply say what is true for you.

The fourth step is really three very important things you can do to actually begin setting up that reconciliation. The first is to ask yourself **who besides you in your family system is in some kind of recovery?** Who besides you would have any kind of understanding of what you are talking about or why you are doing this work?

The second thing you can do is to **gather your resources before you begin.** Rather than getting your family together, plopping down in the middle of them, and demanding that everyone change, form a little group with any other recovering persons in your family, if such persons exist. For however long it takes—and it may take months and months—be in communication with them. Strategize with them. See if they are as interested in some kind of reconciliation effort as you are. Begin to talk to them about how you might go about it. This will form a core of strength within that family system.

The third thing you can do is to **work out a specific strategy with them to actually pull off the reconciliation event.** With them, decide *when* might be the best time for this to happen. With them, decide just how many people are going to be involved in this meeting. Perhaps some people in your family, because of the severity of their problems, shouldn't be there at this point. Perhaps if they're there, as you might very well know, they are going to do absolutely everything in their power to wreck the event. And they may be the ones who have all the power in the first place. So who is going to be there? Where and what time is it going to happen? It may be that just to have it anywhere is not to your advantage. Where is the best, most neutral place to have this reconciliation take place? Now, what is the best way to proceed? Who is going to start first? When you strategize the event, you don't leave it to chance. You stack your deck every way you conceivably can.

An important part of the psychology and the actual art of setting up these reconciliations—which are not totally different from chemical dependency interventions—is that you *get specific*. If you are not specific, you leave too much room for hurt feelings or letting delusion and denial take over. If you are going to say, "Many times in my past I felt that I didn't really count," you are watering down your message. You need to get very specific about the times you felt that way and why you felt that way. Be prepared enough to say, "When you guys always went to my brother's ball games and you never once came to my recitals, you never once came to my plays, you never once came to my debates, it hurt my feelings more than you'll ever know. I'll tell you what I took out of that was that he counted and I didn't." That's specific. Give examples and be as precise as you can.

Another important part of working out this strategy is to ask yourself, "What is my hoped-for result?" What will make the reconciliation event a success in your eyes?

What are your criteria of success? You need to know this before you start. Are you looking for some kind of concrete action to be taken? For example, do you want someone to go into treatment? Or do you want someone to apologize to you? What is the hoped-for goal? Perhaps the goal is *not* to focus on any kind of response at all from your family system. The hoped-for goal simply may be to speak the truth, no matter what happens. The goal for you may be simply to say what you have to say. *But you must understand your goal,* whatever it is. Maybe there is still some kind of behavior going on in your family system that absolutely needs to be confronted and stopped. If that's the goal, you have the best chance of making that happen if you have a core of strength not only from you but from any other recovering people that may exist in that system. Get as much strength as you can.

The fifth step toward reconciliation is to **consider ahead of time whether or not a professional third party may be needed.** As you talk with people in your group, you may very well come up with the names of counselors who understand reconciliation, codependency, and shame, and who can work with you to help set this up in the best manner possible. Especially if the reconciliation involves more than you and one other person, you may need a neutral outsider. Without an uninvolved third party there, your reconciliation may well get to be an organized street fight. It may be extremely helpful to meet with a professional counselor for a few sessions to help you get your expectations in order, to get your motivations clear, to better define your version of success.

Preparing for a reconciliation is very difficult work. You don't want to walk way from a reconciliation feeling that it's been a failure when, in fact, it may have been a wonderful success. What do you hope to get out of it? A professional helper can be a scorekeeper, a referee, somebody who has the skill and the ability and the emotional distance, perhaps, to pull back when the action heats up and say, "Now wait a minute. What you are saying doesn't sound like what this person said. Would you please repeat back to this person what you think you heard?" Many, many times what others hear you say is not what you said at all. What they hear you say is that they were terrible parents, that they didn't care, that they were abusive and mean every hour of every day. If there is no third party who can call a time-out and pull people apart and keep the train on the track, the whole meeting may become a runaway locomotive hurtling toward disaster.

In some cases, if your family system is open

enough, you and the counselor can set up the reconciliation by mail. When people live in many different parts of the country, homework can be given out. Tasks can be assigned so that the people involved can think about, reflect on, and write about certain issues before the reconciliation actually happens. If you do need a counselor, it's not a good idea to start the family meeting and have the counselor suddenly appear, when nine out of the ten people there have no idea where the counselor came from. Everybody there needs to know that a counselor will be involved, that a third party is going to be there.

The sixth step in getting ready for the reconciliation is to understand fully that **expectations are everything.** Frustration is always relative to expectation. If your expectations are unrealistic, there is no doubt at all that you will come out of there frustrated. The success of the attempt that you are making cannot depend on *their* acceptance and on *their* response. The success of what you are trying to do is primarily based on the fact that *you made the attempt.* If you know that you have legitimately and honestly done everything you could, you have advanced the degree of spirituality in this world. If you have done everything you possibly could to break through that family system and raise it to a healthier, more loving, more spirit-filled family, you have done your job. That's success for you regardless of what other people's outcomes from the meeting are.

It can only help to list your expectations one more time. What do you really think will happen as a result of all this effort and preparation? Share your honest thoughts with someone. Before you try to reconcile with anyone else, before you go home to confront mother, father, brother, sister, whoever it may be, share your expectations with someone else. What do you expect is going to happen? Get some feedback from your support system ahead of time.

One woman came back to her group after a disappointing reconciliation attempt and asked, "Why am I always surprised that fig trees have figs?" Of course she was talking about the false hope she had that her family would somehow be different than they ever were before. But fig trees do have figs; they don't have apples. If you go to an apple tree looking for figs, you're going to be disappointed. And if you go to a fig tree looking for apples, you're going to be disappointed. If your family system is not in recovery, they may not understand what you are talking about or what you are trying to do. They may not respond at all the way you dreamed they would. But if your expectations are realistic, *you are not going to be destroyed*. You are not going to be damaged. That's the important thing.

The seventh step is for you to **check out your motives.** Expectations depend to a great extent on what your motivation is. Now, think about this. Is your motivation simply revenge? Is it to punish the offenders of the past by rubbing your recovery in their faces? At this stage of the game, maybe the power has shifted into your hands and, by God, you are going to make them feel as bad as you felt years ago. You are going to accuse them and attack them and in that way unburden yourself of a whole lifetime of pain. If that's your motivation, you are going to be very successful when you go in there with bats swinging and guns blazing. No doubt you can make everybody bleed. But naked revenge is not very worthy, and it is probably not going to make you feel better for long.

Another motivation you may have is to prove that you are free. This is a legitimate motivation. With this motivation, it's not always necessary to look for or get any positive response from the others. The point of the meeting is to prove to yourself that in the face of this punishing family system, you can speak the truth, you can share with them what you really think and what you really feel. The sucess is in accomplishing just that. Your confrontation doesn't have to be vindictive; it doesn't have to be vengeful. You're not out to hurt anyone. Your goal is to stop your habitual stuffing and people-pleasing by finally telling those people exactly how you feel and exactly the way it was for you.

A third motivation may be to invite these people to a level of breakthrough. By talking as straight as you can, you invite and encourage them to be healthier and more whole than they are now, if they so choose. The difference between an invitation and a showdown, of course, has a lot to do with how you approach them, how you talk to them, what you say, and how you say it.

What is your motivation? To a large extent your motives will dictate what your real agenda is. Is it for your sake and for your freedom? Is it to punish them? Is it to invite them to something better? What is your agenda? What your agenda is will become crystal clear when you get honest about what your motive is. Why do you really want to do this?

As tempting as it is to fantasize about a successful reconciliation, you may be thinking right now that, in your case, there is little real basis for hope. As you go through these exercises, you may sadly but certainly realize that there has been no growth or recovery in any of your family members. *But remember that tough love has made many miracles hap-*

pen. Maybe people in your family are just waiting for someone to open the door. Perhaps they aren't able to take the first step and reach out. But if you approach them in a loving, healing manner, it may be that they're only too ready to respond in a way that would absolutely amaze you. Tough love has generated many, many wonderful and surprising turnarounds in this world. So think long and hard. Even if it seems that there is no real hope for a fairy tale reunion, for your sake— as long as it is not terribly dangerous and detrimental to your own recovery—you may want to try a reconciliation.

Lastly, any such difficult effort as this requires support. What is your support system? Who do you get strength and feedback from *before* you make your reconciliation attempt, *while* it is going on, and *after* it has happened? There's just no substitute for adequate support if you are going to successfully carry this out. And, again, success is not dependent on their response; it's dependent on your response, your preparation, your motivation, and your realistic expectations.

6 ✿ ✿ ✿

Clear and
Present Anger

All of our problems with anger aren't rooted in the past. No matter what we decide to do or not to do about our long-term issues, the irritations and annoyances of daily life must be dealt with on a daily basis. Life is lived in the short term, after all, and intelligent life management requires us to take care of the splinters and bee stings as well as our deadlier disabilities.

Most of us are all too conscious of our regular and relentless expressions of anger. We may feel furious or frozen, sarcastic or slow burning, petty or punitive, on a fairly habitual basis. Often, it's a combination of "anger hooks" that team up to provoke the angry response. Perhaps it's an especially long commute *plus* an endless line at the supermarket that pushes us over the edge. Or an argument with a surly child *in addition to* discovering a dent in the new car. As one friend confided to another, "It isn't the lions and tigers that get to me—it's the ants."

The anger hooks that regularly snag us are usually small hooks, and they're on the surface. They have nothing to do with unresolved family of origin issues. They aren't part of any massive conspiracy against us, and they aren't layered over with disguises or scar tissue. They're as nonambiguous and nonmysterious as rain on a picnic. But that doesn't mean they can't diminish the quality of our lives. Peace of mind can be "pebbled to death" as well as crushed with one giant boulder. That's why it's important to understand the present as well as the past when we're trying to come to grips with the debilitating effects of anger in our lives.

Areas of "clear and present" anger might be said to fall into three general categories.

The World

We need to go no further than the daily news reports to wonder if the world has gone mad. Just click on the TV and think about what you're seeing and hearing. What is it but an onslaught of evidence that injustice is commonplace, greed is fashionable, and the power mad are firmly in control? At least on a subliminal level, the triumph of style over substance makes any thoughtful person angry. Which is not even to mention news of cataclysmic natural disasters, like earthquakes and floods, all over the world. Nor even "local highlights" such as a newborn baby found in a dumpster or an old folks' home burning down. The repetition of such events is constant, and so is the hammering on our psyches. Unless we shut down to it completely, which is practically impossible, "news of the world" is a daily dose of horror and helplessness. Talk about a setup for anger!

The Local Environment

Most of us work at imperfect jobs with imperfect bosses and co-workers. We live with imperfect people in imperfect houses. We buy imperfect food and clothing at imperfect stores, which we drive to in imperfect cars on imperfect roads. We're often surrounded by music we don't like, conversations we don't want to hear, and people we don't want to see. The rent goes up; the car breaks down. The garden fails; the weeds flourish. A family of screamers rents the house next door. The cobwebs in the corner—which only we are ever going to notice—distract us from our few moments of relaxation with a murder mystery. Then the telephone rings (not for us). Then there's a knock on the door (not for us, either, unless it's someone selling something). Is there no letup in the relentless rat-a-tat-tat? It doesn't seem so. Consistent serenity is a major achievement in the midst of so many buzzing flies.

The Personal

Small sorrows and workaday woes can be classed with "disasters at a distance" when we're talking about anger hooks. They are so close and so familiar that we're almost comfortable with that kind of discomfort. And other kinds of disasters are almost too remote for reaction; after all, *we* aren't starving in the Sudan, and *we* can't personally put an end to greedy power brokering. But there are personal holocausts that absolutely can't be accommodated with rationalization or good humor or philosophizing. These are events and situations that strike right through our protective strengths and pierce our innermost selves. Many times such events are too intimate for telling; words like "outrage" don't begin to describe how we feel. Often these situations befall us randomly— without rhyme, reason, or warning. Sometimes the effects are irreversible. In the aftermath, our lives are never the same.

Devastating illness or injury to ourselves or our loved one is as infuriating as it is exhausting. If the loss of health is chronic, the very shape and form of our lives is dismantled. The building blocks that once added up to *us* have to be reexamined one by one, some have to be discarded as useless from here on out, some are simply shattered beyond repair. Who wouldn't be angry about starting from scratch, forced to create a new, adapted self, when a lifetime of effort has been invested in the old one? In lesser degree, this daunting task—and the rage that goes with it—is the lot of people who no longer have jobs or identities that were central to their self-definition. They may be forcibly retired executives, permanently "displaced" middle managers, or middle-aged women whose husbands have decided they don't want to be married anymore. In all such circumstances, "what was" is taken away, lost, no longer part of the picture. "What is" is unthinkable and "what may be" is an unknowable phantom of the distant future. *Who wouldn't be angry?* That fate should deny us yachts and jewels is one thing; that we should be denied *who we are* (the only self we know how to be) is quite another. Just as with hidden anger, it's the unfairness that scalds deepest when

the "known self" meets up with dynamite.
What could be more unfair?

And all personal devastations don't have to
register ten on the Richter scale to qualify as
genuine devastations. There is no therapy or
meaningful solace in making glib or superficial comparisons between the "better" or
"worse" wounds of two fallen soldiers. We
have no moral obligation to trivialize our own
suffering because other people are suffering
greater losses than our own. Beyond a quick
"reality check" for perspective, this kind of
thinking is useless; it doesn't help them *or* us.
When your misery cup is full, it's full.
Thoughts like, "I shouldn't feel this way. I
have it so much better than many others," or
"I have no right to complain. I should be able
to rise above this," may very well be the same
old voices from the past that told us our righteous anger didn't count *then* and are still
telling us that it doesn't count *now*.

Anger over intimate, personal issues that
register, say, only a five on that mythical devastation scale, can still shake our lives apart.
Doing daily battle with a defiant teenager can
make us dream of hand grenades. Love relationships that aren't nearly loving enough can
and do shrivel our souls, leaving us embar-
rassingly and resentfully naked to hypersen-
sitivity. Financial difficulties can crush our
pride and make us not only beggars, but

seething, vengeful beggars. Being ignored, dismissed, or in any way treated as nonpersons on the job or in our communities can be mortifying. These and many other intensely personal situations—the death of a beloved pet, the gradual and dismaying loss of youth and beauty—are not such small potatoes that we "ought" to be able to overlook them, brush them off, or simply take them in stride without flinching. Even if they're not "the worst thing that ever happened to us," they *are* happening to us, again and again and again. They grind us down and wear us away. And whether or not some internalized judge grants us entitlement, *we are mad* about a lot of the pain that afflicts our personal lives.

Beyond acknowledging that it exists, what can we do about the "clear and present" anger in our lives? As indignant as we may be, we know that the world will go on as it is, even if we cover our ears during the nightly news. And unless we win the lottery and can stay on the move in luxury, the local environment can't be expected to change much either. That same lottery jackpot might also cut us some slack—or buy us some fancy distractions—from *some* of our personal pain. But for the most part, money can't buy what we most need. It can't buy love or respect or wholeness or health. It can't turn back the clock or end atrocities. It can't bring the dead back to life. So what *can* we do?

As always, when we point the finger of blame, in this case at the anger makers in our lives, three of our fingers are pointing back at us! As always, the things we can change have a lot more to do with us than with them, a lot more to do with our insides than with their outsides. In other words, we may not be able to stop the rain, but we sure as heck can wear a raincoat. Or to put it another way, we can learn better ways to protect ourselves, lessen our vulnerability, and thus limit the damage caused by the clear and present anger in our lives.

Attitude is the key ingredient in "anger-proofing" our daily serenity and sense of well-being. What are our habitual attitudes toward ourselves, others, the unknowable future, and the plodding sameness of the everyday? Our characteristic attitudes are the glasses we use to view reality. Are we unwittingly looking out through attitude lenses that are as smudged and murky as basement windows? Our accustomed attitudes are mind-sets that continuously—and largely unconsciously—interpret what's going on outside of us. These mind-sets decide whether something is a big deal or just a little deal. To a greater degree than we'd like to think, these knee-jerk mind-sets and not our conscious intelligence tell us whether a provocation warrants a moment of irritation or a month of torment.

Some habitual attitudes actually *magnetize* angry feelings. Three of these typical mind-sets are outlined below. Do any of them sound familiar?

"Others have more, and an easier time getting it, than I do."

This unfortunate and self-defeating predisposition is set up by long-term "loser" thinking. Often the passivity and paralysis of victimhood is behind this. We who come to the table of life with this attitude in place are obviously ineffective negotiators. We give away most of what we have before the bargaining even begins. In effect, we deal ourselves out of the game every time. Alternate versions of this attitude go like this: "I never have any luck." "Success isn't really possible for people like me." "I get all the bad breaks." "If I'd had more advantages as a child, I might have had a chance." "It's better not to expect too much."

"The world revolves around me."

Those of us who make all our moves out of this position rarely have any idea that this is the case. But our self-centeredness is a direct result of our failure to recognize the commonality of human experience. We live in an empathy vacuum and consequently find it very difficult to understand other people's interests or motives. Even random and completely nonpersonal events are mistranslated in terms of ourselves alone. One root cause of this attitude may be the directly or indirectly delivered past message that, "You don't count." Other versions of this attitude include, "I'm not going to stand for this. No one can mess with me and get away with it"; "They're out to get me"; "They're jealous of me"; "If I don't look out for Number One, no one else will"; or "I'm the only one around here who has any sense."

"I'm at the end of my rope. I can't take any more."

This attitude is often a symptom of spiritual and physical fatigue. Any thought of mounting a campaign against life's hardships brings on overwhelming feelings of hopelessness and helplessness. Any breeze that blows is seen as an ill wind, if not a killing frost. Such exhaustion, of course, is a fertile field for wildly magnified hurt feelings, suspicions, and grievances of every sort. Those of us who feel this way were probably taught that regeneration and "going the distance" are storybook fantasies. We believe that, ultimately, collapse and defeat are the only *real* realities. Variations on this theme include, "I hate God, fate, you for grinding me down"; "I blew it long ago. It's too late now"; "I'm going to make you just as miserable as I am"; and, "No one else cares whether I live or die—why should I?"

Think about the anger-magnetizing mind-sets described above. Isn't it crystal clear that these are *setups for upset*? Far more than the specific, anger-causing situations themselves, aren't such negative mind-sets the big problem behind all those smaller problems? Think about what would happen if you put on a blue serge suit before walking across a cotton field. What would your suit look like when you got to the other side of the field? What else could you expect?

In life as in science, *the experimenter is always part of the experiment*. There's no arguing the fact that our mind-sets determine how we deal with daily provocations to anger. The irritating situations, like the floating wisps of cotton, may not be under our control—but the self we present to an irritating environment is. Which of our attitudes are like a blue serge suit?

Handicapping Attitudes

Handicapping attitudes vary widely, of course, but the following checklist offers some fairly common denominators. As you read through the list, think about some of the most recent angry episodes in your life. Which descriptions ring a bell or perhaps make you feel a little nervous or defensive? Pinpointing specific areas of vulnerability can give you specific ideas for "demagnetizing" yourself.

Faulty Observation

Rush to judgment before all the facts are in; impatient; prejudice; blinded by self-justification; give too much credence to gossip and eavesdropping

Hypersensitivity

Emotional "startle reflex" that prohibits rational thought; chronically thin skin; inability to relax; literal-minded; sense of isolation and alienation

Unpreparedness

Never have a plan of your own; unskilled at prioritizing and shifting gears; often taken by surprise at predictable happenings; consistently neglect "homework" or any independent search for information

Lack of Ventilation

Life-style is often too sedentary and too routine; overvalue control and distrust spontaneity; always hold back in intimate relationships; divert tears from outside to inside; find company of family members "safer" than friends

Fun-Starved

Business and duty are total preoccupations; knee-jerk resentment at other people's playfulness; nervous on vacation; won't "dance" but hurt at not being asked; unsuccessfully feigns jolliness; would rather stay home than attend a party

Short-Circuited Spirituality

Insist on own terms when dealing with God; have juvenile notions of being a "good girl or boy"; only pray in time of trouble; have cold or punitive parents; are deeply angry with God

It's most important at this point, as you make note of any suspicious signs and symptoms, to bear in mind that the goal of this exercise is *not* to stack up a big pile of evidence against yourself. The goal is to build up your immunity to inappropriate, out of control anger. It isn't honest to admit to a wide range of problems you really don't have. Most people don't have twenty-seven significant blind spots; they have two, three, or four. Accurate, specific indentification of the ones you have is what's going to make the difference. Think about it. Only a fool would go to the dentist and say, "I've got a toothache in there somewhere, so drill 'em all!"

Positive Attitudes

Positive, anger-deflecting attitudes have as many commonalities as negative attitudes do. As a quick check, ask yourself the following questions about your own automatic attitudes toward life as a whole, not just its darker side.

Am I blind to my blessings?

Oh, how quickly human nature takes the pluses for granted and dwells on the minuses! Do we have adequate food, clothing, and housing? Millions of the hungry and cold in the world can only dream of the full stomachs we assume to be our right. Do we have enough health to keep going? A short walk down the hall of any hospital is enough to remind us that health is a precious gift that won't always be ours. Are there people who love us? People whose faces light up when they see us coming through the door or hear our voice on the telephone? Again, how thoughtlessly we tend to assume that we are "owed" more love than we get. How careless we can be with the irreplaceable people in our lives—as if we are somehow entitled to perfection! **Anger-resistant people are aware of their benefits.**

Am I living too much in the small room of self?

When was the last time we threw open a window on the locked room of our own thoughts? Do we imagine that it's "strong" to avoid sharing? Do we stew in silence? Are we so sure that we know the parameters of our anger-causing conditions so well that we don't need outside input of any kind? No reading for new ideas, no checking out our motives with an experienced, trusted friend? If we consult only our inner monologue of complaint—where will we get fresh insights?

Do we *ever* get out of ourselves and take a look at the rest of struggling humanity (who look a lot like us)? Do we need to make a conscious, albeit uncomfortable, effort to try sweeping with a new broom? **Anger-resistant people are open to the wisdom of others.**

How important are the situations that make us angry?

No one is saying that small things don't count. The paper cuts of life can sting and drive us absolutely crazy. The point is, we need to recognize gradations. Aren't some of the things we complain about fairly inconsequential? Have we developed a habit of snowballing many little gripes into a massive boulder of a grudge? Do we use heavy words to describe light realities; is a wait in line an *inconvenience* or an *outrage*? Do we have only one (explosive) response to a wide range of negative stimuli? **Anger-resistant people consistently prioritize their problems and respond to them accordingly.**

Is "bristling" what we do best?

How much does it take to get our hackles up? Or are they *permanently* up? Chronic defensiveness can turn us into virtual porcupines. The "practice makes perfect" rule implies that the more we flinch, the better we get at flinching. Are we consistently overre-acting? Have we unknowingly built a "style" around cynical comments and smart re-marks? Are we already defensive when we get out of bed in the morning? Are we consis-tently crabby? **Anger-resistant people make a point of practicing cheerfulness whether they're happy or not.**

Are we fantasizing a maximum return on a minimum investment?

Laziness is embarrassing, but the question has to be asked: Are we dreaming instead of doing? Is it reasonable to imagine that fitness will be there on game day if we usually skip practice? Are we angry because we think the rigors of life apprenticeship should already be over? Have we slipped into sloppy self-maintenance *while at the same time* expect-ing success and rewards at every turn? Are we waiting for emotional maturity rather than working for it? **Anger-resistant people maintain their resilience skills as conscien-tiously as they maintain their skills at any-thing else.**

Have we lost the ability to let up and let go?

Have we enjoyed a really good belly laugh lately? Or has the "real world" of drudge and duty blotted out the equally real world of play and celebration? Are we so conscious of burdens to be shouldered and attacks to be fended off that we *never* take off our overalls and put on our party clothes? When was the last time we deliberately took a week or a day or an evening to do nothing but have a good time? Does the free child within us only get let out a couple of times a year—or worse, only by accident? Have we allowed our lives to be divided between work and too tired to work, between sweating and sleeping? Has relief gradually taken over the place that fun used to have in our lives? **Anger-resistant people take time to create opportunities for fun.**

Questions such as these can give us important clues about our vulnerability to anger. In matters of physical vulnerability, it isn't hard for us to understand and accept that a fatigued, malnourished body is a fertile field for infections and degenerative diseases. Doesn't it logically follow that exhaustion and neglect take their toll on our mental, emotional, and spiritual lives as well? Weakened emotional defenses leave us unguarded when hurt feelings creep up on us. Unrecognized mental mistakes continually send us into the wrong battles at the wrong time. Spiritual starvation makes us hungry enough to eat the poisoned fruit of righteous self-justification, bitterness, and revenge. Mental, emotional, and spiritual flab won't work any better than bodily flab will. And as we all know—getting in shape is an inside job. No one can do it *for* you, and no one can do it *but* you.

Anger-causing circumstances will always be with us. The daily arrows will come our way, as will an occasional bazooka blast, and there's not a thing in the world we can do to stop them. But we *can* shrink ourselves as targets. We can learn to recognize predictable patterns and steer clear of predictable blowups. We can start implementing our own plan of action rather than reacting to someone else's. We can stop rushing out into the whirlwinds of the world when we're naked, hungry, alone, and tired.

Disarming Our Anger

The principles behind anger disarmament, as behind all emotional management, are almost too simple to be taken seriously in an age so dazzled by complex technologies. Like many rock-solid truths, they're not particularly snappy or catchy or clever. They don't have an avant-garde, revolutionary ring to them because most of these guidelines are old—as old as human experience. They aren't the result of current research, nor are they the latest success formula concocted by an articulate guru on the talk show circuit. But we should be aware that these truths, the ones that "go without saying," often do go—right through one ear and out the other. Perhaps we would be wiser, calmer people if we held on to them a little while, turned them over in our minds, and tried to find the vein of gold that made these nuggets of truth so valuable to past generations.

One such overlooked truism is that we must be *prepared for joy* if we wish to be more joyful people. To this end, some people keep a journal of all the good things going on in their lives. Some keep a scrapbook of cartoons, humorous stories, and upbeat news events. All are *on the lookout* for the positive and the beautiful in the midst of the negative and the ugly. Some days they have to dig for it—that's what preparation is—but they find what they're looking for because that's where their attention is focused.

People who make a daily habit of *encouraging other people* are energized by spending that energy. Compliments don't cost anybody anything. And giving others what *we* need somehow turns the tables on the wear-and-tear process. We become active agents of betterment rather than passive pincushions. The dynamic is so simple it's startling. Rather than watch each other being mugged by stress, we halt the battering with nothing more than a personal acknowledgment or a kind word. Over time, such repeated good deeds reveal themselves as what they are— good deeds to ourselves—for we become what we habitually do.

Another old but evergreen truism has to do with good intentions and procrastination. If we recognize that change is necessary and that someone needs to get it started, *what are we waiting for?* Cliches like, Strike while the iron is hot, and A stitch in time saves nine, have lasted through the ages because they mean something. Today, the wording may fall flat, but there's nothing old hat about a bias for action. People who deal well with anger are people who are taking care of business as it comes up. They know that they share some responsibility for the aggravating way things are, so they don't waste time denying it. They get on with one task before it becomes a whole series of tasks. They don't wait for ideal conditions before they make a move. They know that *now* is the only time they can be sure of, so they're willing to chip away at the obstacles they meet instead of fantasizing about blowing them away. The old fable about the race between the tortoise and the hare is a case in point. Inching ahead won out over flash.

What are the specific irritations in our own lives? How appropriate is our degree of response? If inappropriate, what are the underlying issues?

Our search for answers to these questions might also be called the search for serenity. And what has more to say about the nuts and bolts of serenity than the famous Serenity Prayer?

> *God grant me the serenity*
> *to accept the things I cannot change*

Acceptance doesn't mean lying down for abuse or tolerating the intolerable, but it does mean seeing things as they are and acknowledging that what is so, is indeed so. Acceptance doesn't imply inevitable defeat, but forthcoming decision.

The courage to change the things I can

This phrase tells us that courage is not a dreamy-eyed, sentimental notion, but a deliberate decision to get some dirt under our fingernails. How often we use mind games to opt out of work that we know is ours and ours alone! To admit that self-generated change is possible, is to take responsibility and stop hiding out in helplessness.

And the wisdom to know the difference

This phrase reminds us that "smart" and "right" aren't the same thing. Wisdom implies the ability to *unlearn* cherished untruths, if need be. It implies openness to new ways of processing information—perhaps by keeping a journal or candidly sharing our feelings with friends. Wisdom has to do with the lifelong evolution of discernment, not a once-and-for-all grasp of an ethereal skill or concept.

Bearing in mind that attitude always precedes behavior, here are eight concrete steps that are absolutely guaranteed to tune up your attitudes before you move ahead on your journey. If you follow these steps faithfully, your path will lead you to a better place than you are now.

The Eight Steps to Serenity

1. Practice meditation.

You don't have to shave your head or travel to a faraway holy land to lift up your heart in meditation. If you're honestly seeking the presence of God in your life if you're issuing a daily invitation and listening as well as speaking—you're meditating. Even brief moments of meditation, if frequent, are enough to expand your awareness.

2. Get some strong support.

Withdrawal and loneliness are great fertilizers of hurt and anger. As our lives unfold, we need to "tell our story" to people who know who we are and what we're trying to do. We need to find confidants who are not afraid to offer us constructive criticism and suggestions for improvement, and who are also not too detached to give us a hug when we're sad or some nonjudgmental company when we're licking our wounds. "Over the fence" chats with neighbors aren't enough; we need to talk about real stuff.

3. Schedule recreation.

Fun isn't a "freebie" for most adults. Good times must be valued enough to plan and protect. Some of us have to do some hard thinking just to come up with ideas for activities that *might* be fun. We have to *know* what shifts our attitudes to a higher gear before we can actually make it happen. From then on, it takes discipline to ensure that our chosen recreation is regular, not random.

4. Find mind shifters.

Some of us need vigorous physical exercise to take a vacation from our heads. Some of us waft away on music, and some of us on the quiet contemplation of nature. It's important that we know what works for us. Any nontoxic stimulus that breaks the stress cycle gives us a chance to catch our breath. Mind shifters carry us away, even if for just a little while. The self that returns to the fray comes back refreshed and renewed.

5. Keep a carrot in front of you.

Anticipation of future happiness is good for the soul. Having something to look forward to is what makes the going forward worthwhile. Whether these are little treats like a bubble bath or major events like a trip around the world doesn't matter nearly as much as the experience of joyful expectancy. Those of us who are uncomfortable with giving gifts to ourselves will especially profit from "planting carrots in our own path." We need to know that we can provide our own harvest.

6. Take care of your body.

A healthy attitude has a hard time coexisting with an unwell body. It's no secret that our bad health habits will get us if we don't get to them first. Just the smallest redirection of our nutrition and exercise behavior can point us toward new goals and trigger further progress. Taking intelligent care of our bodies makes us look better, think better, and feel better. Even a short daily walk pumps enough oxygen to steady our nerves and lift some mental fog.

7. Spend time with friends.

Our pals may or may not be part of our nuts-and-bolts support system; we don't use them the same way, nor invite them to think of us so objectively. On the contrary, our dearest friends are obligingly blind to our faults and are passionate partisans on our behalf. They usually share our interests and our sensibilities. In no other company are we so free to be ourselves—without roles to play or rules to follow. Our friends, in fact, are our "other selves." How could we get by without them?

8. Make a contribution.

Our own frustrated wants move into perspective when we address ourselves to the dire needs of others. Even in the leanest times, we all have something to give to others—even if it's a card or a phone call. Comforting and whining are incompatible. How hard it is to obey when we tell ourselves to stop bristling! How much easier and more natural it is to gradually let the bristling go because we simply don't have time for it. Energies focused on positives aren't available for negatives. And redefining ourselves as contributors has another wonderful side effect. It steals thunder from the infuriating "victim" self-definition that is behind much of our trouble with anger. It makes us part of the solution rather than the problem.

If the Serenity Steps sound like common sense, mental hygiene principles, it's because they are exactly that. Simplicity is the goal, as well as the path, to feeling okay because we *are* okay. Managing anger—or any other powerful emotion—isn't a trick or a technique we need to "get the hang of." How is effective emotional management even possible if our lives are a jumble of unmanageable parts and pieces? We need *all* the pieces to complete the puzzle and to have a whole picture. We can't very well manage what we don't have or what we're afraid to use. The Serenity Steps ensure that all the bases are touched and all the pieces are available so that they *can* be managed.

Life is short. How much time are we willing to lose to feelings of anger and resentment? Each of us has both the privilege and the responsibility for our own answer. As long as we live, the anger bait will dangle; will we bite or swim on? The choice is ours.

About the Author

Earnie Larsen, a nationally known author and lecturer, is a pioneer in the fields of recovery and personal growth. A nationally recognized authority on helping people make the most of their lives, he is the creator of the concept of Stage II Recovery.

A counselor for over twenty years, he founded the Earnie Larsen Life Management Center, a unique program for discovery and change based on the Stage II recovery process. His bestselling books include *Days of Healing, Days of Joy*; *New Patterns, New Truths*; and *Stage II Recovery*.

✳
"EASY DOES IT, BUT DO IT"
with Hazelden Books

THE TWELVE STEPS TO HAPPINESS *by Joe Klaas*
36787 $4.95

BARRIERS TO INTIMACY: For People Torn by Addictive and Compulsive Behavior *by Gayle Rosellini and Mark Worden*
36735 $4.95

BACK FROM BETRAYAL: Recovering From His Affairs *by Jennifer Schneider, M.D.*
36786 $4.95

LIVING RECOVERY: Inspirational Moments for 12 Step Living *by Men and Women in Anonymous Fellowships*
36785 $4.95

COMPULSIVE EATERS AND RELATIONSHIPS *by Aphrodite Matsakis*
36831 $4.95

CREATING CHOICES: How Adult Children Can Turn Today's Dreams Into Tomorrow's Reality *by Sheila Bayle-Lissick and Elise Marquam Jahns*
37378 $4.99

SHOWING UP FOR LIFE: A Recovering Overeater's Triumph Over Compulsion *by Heidi Waldrop*
37379 $4.99

AGAINST THE WALL: Men's Reality in a Codependent Culture *by John Hough and Marshall Hardy*
37454 $4.99

TALK TRUST AND FEEL: Keeping Codependency Out of Your Life *by Melody Beattie et. al.*
37455 $4.99

MEN'S WORK: How to Stop the Violence That Tears Our Lives Apart *by Paul Kivel*
37939 $5.99

JOURNEYNOTES: Writing For Recovery and Spiritual Growth *by Richard Solly and Roseann Lloyd*
37852 $4.99

FROM ANGER TO FORGIVENESS *by Earnie Larsen*
37982 $4.99

"I WON'T WAIT UP TONIGHT:" What to Do to Take Care of Yourself When You're Living With an Alcoholic or an Addict *by Terence Williams*

37940 $4.99

GRATITUDE: Reaffirming the Good Things in Life
(Hardcover Gift Book and 52 Gratitude Cards)
by Melody Beattie 38020 $16.00

CHANGE IS A CHOICE (Hardcover Gift Book and 52 Change Cards) *by Earnie Larsen* 38021 $16.00

These bestsellers are available in your local bookstore, or order by calling, toll-free, 1-800-733-3000 to use your major credit card.

Price and order numbers subject to change without notice. Valid in U.S. only.

For information about the Hazelden Foundation and its treatment and professional services call 1-800-328-9000. In Minnesota call 1-800-257-0070. Outside U.S. call (612) 257-4010.